T0380756

MOMENTS WITH THE MASTER

A Journal of Devotional Prophetic Poems

David Scott, II

WestBow
PRESS
A DIVISION OF THOMAS NELSON

WestBow Press books may be ordered through booksellers or by contacting:

WestBow Press
A Division of Thomas Nelson
1663 Liberty Drive
Bloomington, IN 47403
www.westbowpress.com
1-(866) 928-1240

Because of the dynamic nature of the Internet, any web addresses or links contained in this book may have changed since publication and may no longer be valid. The views expressed in this work are solely those of the author and do not necessarily reflect the views of the publisher, and the publisher hereby disclaims any responsibility for them.

Any people depicted in stock imagery provided by Thinkstock are models, and such images are being used for illustrative purposes only.

Certain stock imagery © Thinkstock.

ISBN: 978-1-4497-4648-3 (sc)
ISBN: 978-1-4497-4647-6 (e)

Library of Congress Control Number: 2012906593

Printed in the United States of America

WestBow Press rev. date: 05/29/2012

DEDICATION

**This devotional journal of prophetic poems is
dedicated to the Body of Christ.**

"...given to the Body of Christ to edify, exhort, and comfort..."
1 Corinthians 14:3

TABLE OF CONTENTS

POEM	PAGE

POEM	PAGE

POEM	PAGE

PREFACE

One day while I was seeking God for answers to the challenges facing me and my family, the Holy Spirit began to softly speak words to my mind and I began to write. These words came in the form of poems. The very first one was very simple. It was *milk* because I was just beginning. It was...

> *I worked for peanuts*
> *So do you*
> *I put an end to peanuts*
> *So will you.*

My interpretation: Jesus understood and identified with what I was experiencing with my little income and he promised that my situation would soon come to an end. The scripture to support these words was found in 2 Corinthians 8:9

> *'For ye know the grace of our Lord Jesus Christ, that, though he was rich, yet for your sakes he became poor, that ye through his poverty might be rich.'*

As I continued to seek God's face about different challenges, He continued to speak longer and deeper answers through the poems. As I grew, the poems grew from *milk* to *meat*. They revealed His will and specific instructions about how to walk in victory in many different areas of life: such as finances, relationships, health, wisdom, directions, faith, power, etc...

After 10 years of seeking the LORD and receiving over 180 poems, I knew the LORD had quickened to me *Jeremiah 30:2*

> *"Thus speaketh the LORD God of Israel, saying, Write thee all the words that I have spoken unto thee in a book."*

I knew from this command that I was to publish these poems so others could be edified, exhorted, comforted and victorious by them.

After receiving each poem, I researched the Bible to find the Scriptures to support it.

The Bible Translations used for all Scripture References were
the New King James and King James Versions.

Therefore, ALL poems are Scripturally based.
Please note that even though several of the poems may not be in perfect rhyme, they are however, written according to how the author received them from the Lord. He has chosen not to alter them in order to make them fit into a standard pattern.

INTRODUCTION

MOMENTS WITH THE MASTER is a *Journal of Devotional Prophetic Poems.* It is designed not only to be read as a book of poetry, but to be used as an arsenal of the Word of God. These poems are "alive." They are the living Word of God. When spoken aloud and acted upon, situations are miraculously changed.

The author used these poems to navigate him and his family through times of hardship and struggles in his personal life. Over a span of 10 years and even now they continue to provide him with wisdom and direction from the Lord. They help him to be victorious in every walk of life. Every poem is built upon the written Word of God.

This Journal of Devotional Prophetic Poems can be enjoyed at three different Levels:

Level 1 – read for pleasure
Level 2 – read and meditate
Level 3 – read, meditate, and study

Level 1 – Readers selectively read poems of their choice and enjoy.

Level 2 – Readers select specific poem(s) and meditate on how this poem applies to their situation. They may also highlight, underline, and/or jot down notes on the page.

Level 3 – Readers use Level 2 + M.U.B.A. (*Meditate, Understand, Believe, Act*) Worksheets located in the Appendix of this Journal. These poems can be used for personal situations and/or for general Bible study.

Yea Do I Come, Yea Do I Stand

Yea do I come, yea do I stand,
Walk with Me to the Promised Land.

Yea do I come, yea do I stand,
I AM God, thou art man.

Yea do I come, yea do I stand,
Put down the flesh, take My hand,
Put down the flesh, put on the new man.

Yea do I come, yea do I stand,
Put praise on your lips and a sword in your hand.

Yea do I come, yea do I stand,
The one true God, defending My man.

Yea do I come, yea do I stand,
Put down your pursuits, follow My plan.

Yea do I come, yea do I stand,
The God of all creation, the God of this land
Victorious for all who heed My command.

Scripture References:
Romans 13:14
Psalm 149:6

Quality Time

The things that I say to you get lost in your mind,
That's why it's so important for us to have quality time.

Scripture References:
Matthew 26:40

The Altar

By coming to the Altar, I have changed your heart,
You have received forgiveness and made a new start.

Scripture References:
1 John 1:9

I Am The LORD – I Change Not

I am the LORD – I change not-
Hast thou forgotten…from where I brought you out?

I am the LORD – I change not-
Protecting my sheep from fear and doubt.

I am the LORD – I change not-
Protecting my sheep from famine and drought.

I am the LORD – I change not-
Holy I am without wrinkle or spot.

I am the LORD – I change not-
Bringing you to a place without fear and doubt.

I am the LORD – I change not-
Helping you to carry My plans out.

I am the LORD – I change not-
Loving My children, helping them out.

I am the LORD – I change not-
You are children of light – cast darkness out.

I am the LORD – I change not-
Loving each one of you with My arms about.

I am the LORD – I change not-
You are gaining in faith…casting out doubt.

I am the LORD – I change not-
Greater am I within you than he who is without.

Scripture References:
Malachi 3:6

HOPE

Hope so true is built on Me.
Hope for those who trust in Me.

Hope for those who seek My face,
Who lay aside weights and win the race.

Hope eternal for the people of this land,
Who walk with Me and take a stand.

Hope of eternal life with joy and peace.
From striving in their own works they must cease.

Hope for Me – Hope for you-
Hope for those who walk in truth.

Hope is the anchor of your soul-
In the face of adversity dare to be bold.

Hope gets substance from your faith,
Use them together for your way of escape.

Trust in Me and don't give up hope.
I'm with you in the boat;
I'm at the other end of your rope.

Scripture References:
Hebrews 11:1,6 Hebrews 12:1 Hebrews 6:19 Matthew 8:24

My Plans

Repentance says, "Come to the altar,
My Blood will cleanse you when you falter."

Is it not I who gave you forgiveness?
To cover your path when you fall into weakness?

Since the beginning of time,
I have planned your course,
Molding and shaping you
For My plans not yours.

Stay in My Word.
Commune with Me.
My plans for you will become clear to thee.

Scripture References:
1 John 1:7
Ephesians 1:4,5
Romans 9:21

Restoration

In the beginning, I created My man-
With dominion and authority
In My place…he did stand.

Subduing the earth and all that's within,
Communing with Me as My personal friend.

All was well until the serpent came in
And took from My man all I gave him.

I needed a way to restore man's position;
Someone to take his punishment,
To take his perdition.

Another man or an angel
Simply would not do.
The best that I have
I gave to you.

Jesus is made unto you
Righteousness and redemption.
For the debt you should pay
You have received exemption.

Follow Him now and receive restoration-
Out of the grips of sin as a new creation.

Recreated in Christ Jesus
To rule and reign.
Restored to dominion and authority
By the power of His Name.

Scripture References:
Genesis 1:26-28, Genesis 3:1-8, John 3:16, 1 Corinthians 1:30
Romans 5:17, Mark 16:17, 18

Prayer

Prayer is the accelerator that keeps
You moving in the right direction.
I have given it to you
Out of My love and affection.

I desire you to use it to commune with Me.
I desire you to use it to listen to Me.
You ought to always pray and not faint-
That is not the life I desire for My saints.

Prayer is the foundation
Upon which to build your life.
It gives you joy and peace
Instead of stress and strife.

It is part of your armor
Although sometimes neglected;
If you choose to leave it off,
How will you be protected?

Pray to Me in the Name of My Son-
The things you desire will definitely come.

The fervent prayer of My children availeth much,
Why do you neglect a gift
As powerful as such?

One who does not <u>use</u> his weapon
Is as vulnerable to the enemy
As one who does not <u>have</u> a weapon.

Scripture References:
Luke 18:1 John 16:23-24

The Wicked, I

For the wicked do prosper
And live well in your sight;
But it will not help them
On judgment night.

They are fulfilling their role
As I planned it on earth-
To accumulate wealth
That will be transferred to your worth.

They work for you
And they are good at their job.
They hoard it and store it
Where men cannot rob.

That wealth will come to My kingdom
One way or another.
They will either get saved
Or lose it to a brother.

Though they heap up silver as dust
And prepare raiment as clay,
They may prepare it
But the just shall wear it.

Scripture References:
Proverbs 13:22, Ecclesiastes 2:26,
Deuteronomy 8: 18, Job 27: 16-17

The River

There is a river
That flows from My throne.
It is not for all
But those who are My own.

The river will sanctify you
By the word of truth,
To wash away uncleanness
And the lusts of youth.

This river can come
As a mighty rushing wind,
To convict the world
Of their guilt and sin.

It will hover over man
As a dove or flame,
Infilling the man
With the power of that Name.

This river will lead us,
Guide and direct.
If you go the wrong way,
Your spirit…He will check.

This river is not an it
But rather a He.
The Holy Spirit given
To you from Me.

Scripture References:
Revelation 22:1, John 17:17
Acts 2:2-3, Romans 8:14, Ephesians 5:26

The Rock

I AM the Rock of Ages-
Stand on Me.
By walking in My word,
I will sustain thee.

The troubles of the world
Are meant to shake you.
The truths of My WORD
Are meant to establish you.

For solid ground
In the midst of the storm,
Stand on My WORD
You who are reborn.

It is not meant
For thee to go down.
Stand on the ROCK –
The safe and solid ground.

Scripture References:
Matthew 16: 16-18

My Rest

I have designed for My people
To enter into My rest.
For then they would know
How to function at their best.

Israel could not enter in
Because of unbelief.
Will you also be denied
By that same old thief?

I have provided a place
Of great blessing there.
Do not miss out
By holding on to your cares.

Cast them on me
For I care about you.
Enter into rest
And a world you never knew.

Scripture References:
Hebrews 4: 1-10

The Curse

This is the curse
That goeth over the earth.

Into the house of the thief-
Into the house of the swearer-
Into the house
Of the false talebearer.

It shall remain,
Consuming every brick.
It shall remain,
Consuming every wood.
Nothing shall be left
Where that house once stood.

The curse without a cause
Does not come.
It is not for all-
Only for some.

The curse inhabits
The house of the wicked.
Blessings inhabit
The house of the just.

Thank God
Through His son, Jesus-
Those curses no longer apply to us.

Scripture References:
Zechariah 5:1-4
Proverbs 26: 2

My Will

My will for you
Is to come unto Me.
My will for you
Is to be set free.

For those who would bind you
Will no longer be found.
For I have placed your feet
On higher ground.

Look to Me
As you go through the fire.
I will be with thee
No harm will come to your attire.

I AM the LORD,
Who delivers My children.
They should know
I will always be with them.

Fear not the fire!
Fear not the flame!
I will restore your back
From whence you came.

Throw not away your confidence-
Keep your faith high.
I will put an end to this situation.
I will deliver My new creation.

Scripture References:
Psalm 34:19
Isaiah 43:2-3
Hebrews 10: 35

The Just

You are My children.
You are the just.
Born again to righteousness,
In Jesus you did trust.

Living by faith,
Walking with Me,
Walking by My Word,
Not by what you see.

Guided by My Spirit,
Discerning all things,
Reigning in life,
Through Jesus as kings.

You have put away evil,
And all that's wicked in My sight.
You have put on Jesus
And the armor of light.

Scripture References:
Romans 1:17
Romans 5:17
Romans 13:12

The Way

Don't listen to the enemy
When he says there is no way.
A position of hopelessness,
Is not where you want to stay.

Did I not tell you,
I AM the Life, the Truth, and the Way?
The answer will come today-
If you take the time to pray.

Scripture References:
John 8:44
John 14:16

My People

If My people,
Who are called by My name,
Would depend on Me-
Life would never be the same.

If My people,
Would humble themselves and pray,
Direction would come,
They would find the right way.

If My people,
Would turn from their wicked ways,
They would surely see their future
Filled with brighter days.

If My people,
Would walk closely with Me,
I will hear from Heaven
And answer thee.

If My people,
For righteousness would stand,
I will hear from Heaven
And heal their land.

Scripture References:
2 Chronicles 7:14

The Smitten

I am the smitten-
Afflicted of God.
I came out of Jesse;
I am his rod.

Like the rock in the wilderness
Giving life giving water-
I give rivers of living water
To every son and daughter.

Come to Me
All who are burdened and labor.
I will give your rest
And grant you My favor.

Drink of Me
And you will never thirst again.
I stick closer than a brother.
I am your friend.

Scripture References:
Isaiah 11:1
John 7:38
Proverbs 18:24

The Children

You are the children-
Children of light,
Shunning evil ways
Doing what is right.

Come to Me daily
That you may be fed.
The finished work of Calvary,
That is the children's bread.

You have put away
The lusts of your youth.
It pleases Me greatly
When you walk in truth.

Grow up My children
And become as My Son.
Walking in the Word-
A victorious one.

Scripture References:
1 Thessalonians 5:5
Matthew 4:4
3 John 1:4

In My Presence

In My Presence
Is where you should be.
Stop what you're doing
And draw nigh unto me.

In My Presence
Is fullness of joy.
Enter as a little child,
As a little girl or boy.

In My Presence
Is the hiding place,
Under the shadow of the Almighty,
Where no enemy dare give chase.

In My Presence
Is the consuming fire.
I'll burn away your filthy rags
And clothe you in king's attire.

In My Presence
Is life and peace,
Frets and anxieties
Here must cease.

In My Presence
Is light and love,
To guide your way
Says the God above.

Scripture References:
James 4:8, Psalm 16:11, Psalm 91:11
Hebrews 12:29, Romans 8:6

Pure Worship

When worship is right
It is a beautiful sight,
It takes your praise
To glorious heights.

When body, heart and soul
Can function as one,
Praise and worship
Are acceptable to My Son.

Praise escorts you
Into My Presence,
Make sure your worship
Is filled with reverence.

I do inhabit the praise of My people,
Manifesting Myself in gifts and power.
Touching those who diligently
Seek Me in this hour.

Maintain the purity
Of worship and praise.
I will reveal myself to you
All of your days.

Scripture References:
Psalm 100:4, Psalm 22:3, John 4:23

The Anointing

For it is My anointing
Which breaks the yoke.
It is power over demons.
It makes them choke.

Get under My anointing-
Get under the oil,
For striving in the flesh
Is fruitless toil.

My anointing used to be
For prophet, priest and king.
Now for every born again believer,
It is a most sacred thing.

To be used in service
Not for personal gain.
To minister to the world
In the authority of My Name.

It is under the anointing
That My gifts flow.
Gifts of speech and gifts of power-
Gifts that tell you what you need to know.

Operate under the anointing
And not in your own power.
I will manifest Myself
Through you in this hour.

Scripture References:
Isaiah 10:27, Luke 10:19, 1 Samuel 16:13
Luke 11:9-13, Acts 2 :38, Acts 10:45, Acts 1:8, Mark 16:17-19,
1 Corinthians 12:4-11, 1 John 2:27

Freedom

Your freedom has been purchased
By the work of the cross.
You exchanged satan for Jesus,
You have a new boss.

Put off the old man
With his chains that bind.
You are a new creation
That never before existed in time.

For you were helpless slaves
Before I paid your ransom.
Now you are kings and priests
Dressed in righteousness so handsome.

Your minds are free
To understand the truth.
They are no longer blinded
Like the minds of your youth.

Scripture References:
Matthew 20:28, Colossians 1:13, 2 Corinthians 5:17, 1 Peter 2:9

Your Thoughts

Don't occupy your mind
With everything you've heard.
You must screen all your thoughts,
Make them line up with My Word.

When bad thoughts come
Put them to this test,
Like a bird flying over your head-
Run him off before he builds a nest.

Bad thoughts are your enemies,
They must be taken captive.
They must be cast down
And not allowed to remain active.

As a man thinketh in his heart
So is he;
With bad thoughts controlling
Imagine what you might be.

Come up to My thoughts-
Come up to My ways-
Leave the wicked to think on evil
All of their days.

For the carnal mind is against Me,
But the mind of the spirit is life and peace.
Think on the pure, lovely and of good report
And enjoy a new release.

Scripture References:
2 Corinthians 10:5, Proverbs 23:7, Isaiah 55: 7-8
Romans 8:6-7, Philippians 4:8

Turn To Me

Turn to Me
When you cannot see,
I'll light your path
And give your enemy My wrath.

Turn to Me
When you miss the mark,
I'll erase it from your life
So you can make a new start.

Turn to Me
When the enemy comes in,
For My Spirit will raise
A standard against him.

For the angel of the Lord
Is an awesome sight,
He took out 185,000
By himself in only one night.

Scripture References:
Psalm 119:105, Psalm 103:3
Isaiah 59:19-20, 2 Kings 19:35

Husband and Wife

You averted the storm
Which came your way-
Because you were obedient
To get up and pray.

The enemy had planned
To come against your life-
Because of a door
Opened through strife.

The enemy's favorite way
Of disrupting your life-
Is to set himself
Between husband and wife.

Don't allow him there
By holding on to anger.
Forgive each other/commit it to Me,
I'll make your union stronger.

For there is no greater union
On the face of the earth,
Than two who are one flesh
Who know what they are worth.

The power of agreement
Is strongest in you two,
That is why the enemy
Is always after you.

So found your marriage
On the three-fold cord,
You two wrapped around
Jesus – Your Lord!

Scripture References:
Matthew 26:41, Mark 3:24-25, Matthew 18:19-20
James 3:16, Ephesians 4:26-27, Ephesians 5:31, 33, Ecclesiastes 4:9-12

The Transformation

The transformation
Is good for you-
It locks up the old
And releases the new.

Put Agag down
Once and for all-
If you carry him around,
He will cause you to fall.

Once you didn't know
Wrong from right-
The kingdom of darkness
Owned your rights.

Now you are translated
Into the kingdom of the Son-
Forsaking darkness for the light
Of the Mighty Holy One.

You are a new creature
That never before existed,
Your mind is no longer blinded-
Your thoughts no longer twisted.

Look into my Word-
Find out who you really are,
The search may be long,
But it will take you very far.

Scripture References:
Romans 12:2, 1 Samuel 15:33,
Colossians 1:13, 2 Corinthians 5:17

A New Thing

For yet and behold
I will do a new thing.
Stand back and watch
What My mercy shall bring.

For the whole earth shall see
My plan for this age,
In this chapter of life
I am turning a new page.

For the ones who have doubted
Saying there is no God,
Will see My power displayed
As in the days of Moses' rod.

Signs and Wonders
Will fill the earth-
As My power flows
Through the children of the new birth.

Some will say
What manner of man is this?
They will answer-
Lord Jesus is in our midst.

The unbelieving world
Will come to know Me,
By the hands of My children
Who can move and flow with Me.

Scripture References:
Jeremiah 31:31, Habakkuk 2:14, Mark 16:20
Matthew 18:20, Acts 1:8

In A Little While

In a little while
You will find your way.
A new dawn will break forth
Like the light of day.

You will see the course
That I have planned.
Stay in My Word-
Follow My command.

For I have great plans
And things for you to do,
Things you haven't done before-
Things brand new.

Your life will be fulfilling,
A joy to do each day.
Gone will be frustration
And the error of your way.

You will do great things for Me
As I have told you before.
Be patient and study
Until I open the door.

Scripture References:
John 14:19, Jeremiah 29:11,
Ecclesiastes 5:18-19, 1 Corinthians 2: 9-10

Come Up With Me

Come Up! Come Up! Come Up with Me-
Into My presence-
I will take care of thee.

Come Up! Come Up! Come Up with Me-
Out of the darkness and confusion-
Come where you can see.

By the light of My Word
I will show thee great things,
By the power of my Spirit
Ye shall walk as priests and kings.

Come Up! Come Up! Come Up with Me-
Shake off those chains-
Walk as a son who is now set free.

Lose the lower life-
Find the higher life.
Wipe away the spots and wrinkles-
Be adorned as My bride, My wife.

Come Up! Come Up! Come Up with Me-
Seated with Me in Heavenly places,
Find refreshing from the world-
Like a desert oasis.

Come Up! Come Up! Come Up with Me-
Drink of Me – I will sustain thee.

Scripture References:
Ephesians 2:6, Psalm 119:105, Romans 8:14
2 Corinthians 3:17, Matthew 16:25,

Stand Up

Stand Up! Stand Up! Stand Up!
Saith the Lord;
Get your mind, body, and spirit
Into one accord.

Pick up your armor-
Pick up your weapons-
The enemy is under your feet;
On his head start stepping.

You are made to have dominion,
To rule and reign.
You must stand up
And use the Name.

For it is not by might
And not by power-
But My Spirit
Comes victory in this hour.

According to your words
My angels do come near;
Make sure the Word of God
Is what they will hear.

Stand up and fight-
The battle is Mine.
I'll give you the victory
In the fullness of time.

Scripture References:
Ephesians 6:13-14, Genesis 1:26, Zechariah 4:6
Psalm 103: 20, 1 John 5:4

Wait For Me

Wait for Me
And you will see-
All the plans
I have made for thee.

Wait for Me
For I have chosen thee-
To do a great work,
To set men free.

Wait upon Me
As a servant to a king-
Put praise in your heart,
A new song do sing.

Wait upon Me
There is no greater thrill-
Than to carry out My plans
And walk in My perfect will.

Wait upon Me
Alone you will fall.
Wait upon Me
Together we stand tall.

Wait upon Me
I have anointing and power.
Would you minister without these
In this evil hour?

Scripture References:
Isaiah 40:31, Ephesians 1:4, Mark 9:35
John 15:5, Acts 1:8

The Race

The race is for the swift
Not for those who are weighed down.
Eternal life is my gift,
Run to win the glory crown.

Lay aside the sin and weight
Which so easily besets you.
Press on toward the mark and high calling
That Jesus has planned for you.

Drop all baggage from the past-
Look neither to the left nor right.
The image of Jesus
Should be fixed in your sights.

In consistency lies the power
As you run this race,
Day in – Day out in the Word and the Spirit,
I have given you My grace.

So run with confidence
Heads held high,
That great cloud of witnesses
Cheering you from the sky.

Scripture References:
Philippians 3: 13-14, Hebrews 12:2, Hebrews 12: 1

Put Away Agag

Put away Agag,
Cut him no slack.
His one desire in life
Is to hold you back.

You are born again
And now set free.
Put away the old nature-
Draw closer to me.

Mortify the old desire-
Cast down every evil thought-
Your ransom has been paid,
For a price you have been bought.

A monkey on your back
Is more than worldly saying.
My children's old nature
Is constantly slaying them.

Put on Jesus,
His nature, his thoughts-
Then you will see
The victory wrought.

When crises arise
Don't say "What shall we do?"
Stand on My Word,
Act like it's true.

Scripture References:
1 Samuel 15, 1 Peter 1:23, James 4:8, Colossians 3:5, 1 Timothy 2:6
1 Corinthians 6:20, Romans 8:6, Romans 13:14, Ephesians 6:13

The Serpent

When Paul had gathered sticks
And laid them on the fire,
Out of the heat came a viper
And fastened on his hand
With evil desire.

But Paul shook it off,
He shook it into the fire.
For he was clothed with the Lord Jesus,
The Word and Priestly attire.

He felt no harm
From the bite of the snake.
For Paul's very life
The devil could not take.

For I had given him authority
Over the ability of the evil one.
I delivered him through the power
Of the Lord Jesus, My dear Son.

Signs and wonders followed him
Because he believed.
When the serpent took him on,
The serpent had to leave.

Scripture References:
Acts 28: 1-10

My Child

My child is a seed.
He is planted and growing.
He is not perfect,
But I know where he is going.

I will love him-
And forgive him-
When he misses the mark.

I will help him up-
And dust him off-
So he can make a new start.

I will root him and ground him
In the Word of God.
He will be fruitful and budding
Like Aaron's rod.

I will train him up
In the way he should go-
To the devil's temptations
He will learn to say "NO!"

He'll yield his members unto righteousness
Doing the work of the Lord.
My child, Myself, and Jesus
A Might Three-Fold Cord!

Scripture References:
Matthew 19:14, Ephesians 6:4,
Proverbs 22:6, Romans 6:13

The Time Has Come

The time has come
When all My people,
Must make up their minds
To fly like the eagle.

For I created you to ride
Upon the high places of the earth-
To walk as kings and priests
Who know what they are worth.

The time has come
To quit listening to the devil.
By the time he gets through with you,
You have the stature of a pebble.

For he is a liar from the beginning,
The father of it.
As much as you listen to him,
Sometimes I think you love it.

Run him off!
Declare who you are.
Build self-esteem on My Word-
It will take you very far.

Scripture References:
Isaiah 58:14, Ephesians 4:27, John 8:44, James 4:7

The Life of Faith

The life of faith
Is what I've called you to live.
You are the just,
In Me you must trust.

Believe My Word-
Believe My voice-
Faith over fear
Should be your choice.

Don't allow what you see
To control what you do.
Stand on My Word
And act like it's true.

Speak to your mountains,
Cast them in the sea.
The God-Kind of faith
Will do that for thee.

Scripture References:
Galatians 3:11, John 6:29, 2 Timothy 1:7
2 Corinthians 5:7, Ephesians 6:13, Mark 11:22-23

My Favorite Thing

My favorite thing
Is to hear you sing,
Praise and psalms
Unto the King.

My favorite thing
Is that you walk in truth,
Trusting in Me
As parent to youth.

My favorite thing
Is that you exercise faith.
Speak to your mountains
Shouting Grace! Grace! Grace!

Scripture References:
Psalm 22:3, 3 John 1:4, Zechariah 4:7

The Release

You have been released
From the grip of the evil one.
You have been set free
By the sacrifice of My dear Son.

For once upon a time,
You were slaves and didn't know it.
You were debtors to the flesh,
But now you don't owe it.

You have been released
From the spirit of fear.
Boldly rebuke him
When he tries to come near.

You have your release
From the spirit of doubt.
Believe My Word
And cast him out.

Scripture References:
Psalm 107:2, Luke 1:68, Romans 8:12-15

Faith

Faith is the key
That opens the door-
To all of the blessings
That I have in store.

Have faith in Me
And what I will do.
Don't depend on yourself
And what you're used to.

Faith works by love
So watch your walk.
If you don't walk in love,
All you will have is talk.

Faith sees the answer-
Fear sees the problems-
Fear works to destroy you-
Faith works to solve them.

Fear says, "Oh no,
It must be too late."
Faith says, "Oh yes,
My God has made a way of escape."

Fear makes you shake, worry,
Tremble and quiver.
Faith makes you say
"My God had delivered me."

Faith pleases Me
As a Father to a son.
For those who stand in faith,
I will deliver every one.

Scripture References:
Hebrews 11:1, Galatians 5:6, Hebrews 11:6
Mark 5:22-42, 1 Corinthians 10:13, Psalm 91:14-15

Set The Captives Free

Set the captives free
That they may see.
My love and My power
In this late hour.

For they long to be free
From the chains that bind.
They long to see
A better place and time.

For so long
They have been blinded to the truth.
Their minds have been covered
From the days of their youth.

But My Word is a sword
That will cut away the covers,
To bring them into the kingdom
As new sisters and brothers.

My word is a hammer
To beat away oppression,
To free them as My children,
My priceless possessions.

My Word is a water
To wash away the dross,
To clean and renew them,
They will no longer be the lost.

My Word will grow them up
Into holiness and power.
My Word will grow them up
As Mighty Warriors in this late hour.

Scripture References:
2 Timothy 2: 24-26, Hebrews 4:12, Ephesians 5:26
2 Corinthians 3:14, Jeremiah 23:29, Peter 1:23

The Wicked, II

The wicked are overthrown
And are not.
This house shall stand,
For My inheritance is your lot.

They have plotted and schemed
And attempted to bring you down,
But all their plans and devices
I will burn to the ground.

They are against you night and day.
They never cease from their plan.
Remember they did this to me,
When I walked as a man.

Fear them not,
This weapon will not prosper.
They have come in like a flood
But they have run into the Blood.

Speak My Word!
Hear My voice!
Then you will know-
To make the right choice.

Scripture References:
Proverbs 12:7, Psalm 33:10, Isaiah 54:17, Hebrews 4:12-13

Go Forth

Go forth from this place
In the power of My name.
I have prepared a place for you,
Your life will never be the same.

I have turned your mourning
Into gladness and joy.
You will be a like a child
With a brand new toy.

You will find fulfillment
And accomplishment there,
You will be at peace
Working without care.

The talents and skills
That I have placed in you,
Will come forth and blossom
As I manifest through you.

Scripture References:
Mark 16: 15-18, Psalm 30:11, Jeremiah 29:11

The Cup

The Cup! The Cup!
The Cup is for you.
It is born out of My love
And desire to bless you.

Because of the bitter cup
I drank from in the garden,
I now give you a cup of blessing-
If your hearts you will not harden.

It is a cup of blood,
If you are dead in sin-
To give you eternal life,
So you can live again.

It is a cup of water,
If you're dry and you thirst-
To bring back the zeal
That you had at first.

It is a cup of oil,
If you desire the Spirit-
His anointed power,
The enemy does fear it.

It is a cup of fire,
To burn away impurity,
To conform to the image of Him-
Powerful, Pure and Holy.

Scripture References:
John 18:11, John 7:38, Matthew 26:39, Isaiah 10:27,
1 John 1:7, Luke 3:16-17

The Hand Of The LORD

The hand of the LORD
Is an awesome place.
It is a point of no return
Where the enemy dare not give chase.

As Israel came
To the brink of the Red Sea,
They found a place
Where they could no longer flee.

To escape death
At the hand of Pharaoh's rod,
They made the only move they could,
Into the Hand of God.

As the sea parted,
Israel went through.
When Pharaoh saw what happened,
He said, "I think I'll go too,"

Pharaoh's army met death
At the bottom of those sea.
For My hand is for My people –
Not for My enemies.

Scripture References:
Exodus 14:1-31

Come Fly With Me

Come fly with Me
And I will show-
Great things to you
That you must know.

Let go of the sin.
Let go of the weight.
They hold you down
As unnecessary freight.

Let your spirit soar,
Come through the door.
Rising so high-
You can't see the floor.

Come up with Me.
You will see.
Plans and purposes
I have laid for thee.

Scripture References:
1 Corinthians 2:9-12, Hebrews 12:1

The Day is Coming

The day is coming
Thus saith God-
When all of My people
Must give Me their rod.

In this day and time-
You can't walk on your own.
Remember along with the wheat
Many tares are also sown.

It must be that way for a time-
The earth is besieged by crime.
But for My people I provided a haven,
Feed from My Word as Elijah from the raven.

You will find provision
For adverse situations.
You will find life and peace
Instead of days of frustration.

For My Word is your Ark-
Take shelter there.
Put My Word in your mouth
Instead of your cares.

Scripture References:
Exodus 4:1-5, Matthew 13:24-30, 2 Corinthians 4:4
1 Corinthians 10:13, Hebrews 4:12

The Fast

For this is the fast
I have chosen for you-
To loose the band of oppression
The enemy has woven for you.

His plans and his schemes
Look like they will prevail.
Seek Me and turn to Me,
We'll tell another tale.

As in the days of Esther,
It looked like she would not live.
She sought me with fasting-
Into her hand the enemy I did give.

I turned her fasting into feasting,
Mordecai's sackcloth into a robe.
I turned her captivity into royalty
As I did My servant Job.

Pull away from the world,
If only for a time.
I'll turn your mourning into joy
And your water into wine.

Scripture References:
Isaiah 58:6-9, Esther – Chapter 4

It's Not Too Late

In the Name of Jesus
It's not too late.
For your God has delivered you
From this apparent fate.

Though the enemy made it look
Like he really was winning.
What you really have now
Is a brand new beginning.

This weapon formed against you
Will not prosper.
You have spoken against it.
It is no longer on the roster.

You will now receive
That for which you have believed.
For you have executed judgment
Against the enemy.
You were sustained by rivers of living water.
You are planted like a tree.

Don't believe it's too late
When on Me you have to wait.
Do your part – Speak My Word-
Open your mouth – Let your voice be heard.
I will back you up.
I will back up every word.

Scripture References:
Colossians 1:13, Isaiah 54:17
Jeremiah 23:5-6, Psalm 149:6-9

I Have Opened The Heavens

I have opened the Heavens-
Your blessings have been sent.
In case you're wondering where they are,
I'll tell you where they went.

The enemy has stolen them
Right from under your nose.
All because you have failed
To subdue your unseen spiritual foes.

You cannot live a passive life,
Whatever will be, will be.
You must control the wicked one
Or he will continue to rob thee.

The strongman must be bound
And his goods must be spoiled.
For there is one stronger than he,
The greater one is living in thee.

The Blood and the Name
And the Word in your mouth-
Will run him out of your affairs
And send him heading south.

Scripture References:
Malachi 3:10, Ephesians 6:11-13, Matthew 18:18, Luke 11:21-22
Revelation 12:11, Philippians 2:10, James 4:7

The Stone

The stone has been removed;
He is no longer there.
He is risen from the dead
So wipe away the tear.

You now serve a risen LORD,
Not one who only died.
Remember He is alive today,
Not just crucified.

His body and His bones
Are no longer in the grave.
The angel moved the stone-
To sin you are no longer slaves.

Death could not hold Him-
The grave could not keep Him-
Hell could not handle Him-
The devil could not defeat Him.

He is seated today
At the right hand of the throne,
Ruling and resigning
With his foot on the stone.

Scripture References:
Mark 16: 2-7, Revelation 1:18,
Colossians 2:15, Mark 16:19

Grow Up and Go Up

Grow up and go up
Into the deeper things of Me.
Make sure the living waters
Continually feed your tree.

Grow up and see
The things that come against thee,
Are not always your fault,
But come because you're blood bought.

Grow up and see
The only way to victory,
Is to submit to Me,
And resist the enemy.

I have promised you the victory-
You must provide the fight.
Use My Word which releases the Spirit,
Not your own power and might.

Guard your mind at all times
From each fiery dart.
If you don't, your steps to victory
Will never even start.

Once you grow up,
Then you can go up,
Into the deeper things of Me,
You'll be a planted, watered tree.

Scripture References:
Hebrews 6:1-2, 1 Peter 5:8-9, James 4:7,
1 John 5:4, Mark 4:24

My Temple

Take care of My temple
For it houses My Spirit.
Treat it with reverence-
Don't let sin come near it.

My temple is precious,
But it is not redeemed.
Of mind, body and spirit,
It must not lead this team.

It must follow your spirit
After experiencing the new birth,
But your body is important,
It gives you authority in the earth.

Take care of My temple-
With junk food don't trash it.
When sickness comes knocking,
Your immune system will smash it.

My temple must be exercised
To keep it strong and lean.
It profits you in this lifetime
To keep it holy and clean.

Scripture References:
1 Corinthians 6:19-20, Romans 8:14
1 Corinthians 3:17, 1 Timothy 4:7-8

The Earth

The earth is the Lord's
And the fullness thereof.
It belongs to Me
As much as Heaven above.

It was Mine from the beginning,
Although Adam gave it away.
To him who since then has been sinning,
But in the end has no chance of winning.

The earth is the place
Where battle are fought among nations.
Satan can't do anything to Me,
So he goes after My creations.

But you are no longer a creation-
Now you are My child.
You are no longer owned by him-
You have a kingdom lifestyle.

For Jesus took back the earth
Along with the keys of death and hell.
He made a shew of satan openly
And watched as his kingdom fell.

So walk the earth victorious,
As a child of the King of Kings.
Lift your voices glorious
As you praise, worship and sing.

Scripture References:
Psalm 24:1, Haggai 2:8, Luke 4:5-6
I Peter 5:8, Romans 8:15-16
Revelation 1:18, Colossians 2:15

Open Your Eyes

Open your eyes
That you may see-
Things in the spirit
Coming against thee.

For the enemy is plotting
Day and night.
Be strong in Me,
In the power of My might.

Open your eyes
That you may see-
The host of mighty angels
Encamped round about thee.

Open your eyes
That you may see-
Your words control the spirit world,
Not the enemy....nor Me.

Scripture References:
11 Kings 6:17, Ephesians 6:10, Psalm 104:4, Psalm 34:7
Psalm 68:17, Proverbs 18:21, Mark 11:23

The Feasts

It is time to celebrate
The feasts that I have given.
Don't forget your heritage
All you who are My children.

As I took you out of Egypt
And brought you to the Promised Land,
The death angel did PASSOVER you,
You are born again as a new man.

I bestowed upon you My Spirit,
The Holy Ghost and fire,
From this day of PENTECOST
An infilling of power you did acquire.

Restore the singing, the dancing,
And the highest levels of praise,
For now all of you can enter the TABERNACLES
And be in My presence all of your days.

Scripture References:
Exodus 12:21-23, Acts 2:1-4, Acts 15:16

The Truth

The truth will set you free,
But only to the degree-
That you have revelation
Of your rights as a new creation.

It is only the truth you know,
That will free you to go-
Higher and higher into the Kingdom,
Learning and growing as a skillful one.

The truth never changes,
It is the same for all eternity.
Your circumstances are simply facts;
They can change very quickly.

Use the truth
To change the facts.
Look how it worked
In the Book of Acts.

It works the same today,
Even in this hour.
My people are void of speech-
My truth has not lost its power.

Scripture References:
John 8:32, Hosea 4:6, 2 Corinthians 4:17-18, Mark 11:23

Rise Up

Rise up and shine,
And act like you're Mine.
The righteous may fall,
But he gets up seven times.

Rise up and shine,
For your light is Divine.
Let your light shine,
There is coming a better time.

Where you are
Does not determine who you are.
Let who you are
Determine where you are.

Don't stay under the circumstances,
I did not create you there.
I put all things under your feet
Rise up and throw Me your cares.

Rise Up!
You have to stand
For things to be under your feet.

Rise Up!
You have to stand
In order to go to places and
People I want you to meet.

Rise Up!
I said I'll never leave you
But I'm not lying down.

Rise Up!
I said I'll stand with you
If you'll stand your chosen ground.

Scripture References:
Isaiah 60:1, Proverbs 24:15-16, Matthews 5:15, Ephesians 1:22
Ephesians 6:13, Romans 16:20, Hebrews 13:5

Don't Bow Your Knee

Don't bow your knee
To the things of this world.
All will bow to Me,
Every man, woman, boy, and girl.

Why would you bow your knee
To something under your feet?
Keep your foot on him,
Don't let him run your street.

How can I bruise satan
Shortly under your feet?
When My power through you should crush him,
I find …he's gone out to eat.

Walking about going to and fro,
Seeking whom he may devour.
Accusing them, deceiving them because they don't know
Their inheritance in Jesus, their place, their power.

Resist him and all of his wiles.
Cast him out of all of your affairs.
Speak to him – Tell him you're My child.
Inform him – You no longer have a care.

Tell him you read the back of the book.
Tell him you know the end of the story.
Tell him his keys Jesus just took.
Tell him - to <u>God Be The Glory</u>!

Scripture References:
Isaiah 44:17-19, Isaiah 45: 23, Ephesians 2:5-6, Ephesians 1: 19-23
Romans 16:20, John 8:44, Mark 16:17
1 Peter 5:7-9, Mark 11:23, Revelation 1:18

The Wait Is Over

The wait is over,
Go in and possess the land.
The victory is yours,
You overcame because you took a stand.

The wait is over,
It's time for walls to come down.
The wait is over,
You have earned the victor's crown.

The wait is over,
Go and plunder the enemy.
He is ready to fall,
He cannot stand against thee.

The wait is over,
Go and indulge in the spoil.
Your time of standing and standing
Was not fruitless toil.

The wait is over,
The victory is now.
He has no choice but to flee.
At my Name he must bow.

Scripture References:
Ephesians 6:13, James 1:2-4, Matthew 12:29, Philippians 2:10

My Trees Must Be Watered

My trees must be watered,
To survive this barren earth.
If not, they will wither and dry up,
They will be useless and of no worth.

My trees must be watered,
Or they will not grow strong.
They will be weak and sick
All their life long.

My trees must be watered,
If they are to produce fruit.
They must be watered in abundance
From the branches to the root.

My trees must be watered,
They must also be planted.
Firmly established in My house
So their views won't get slanted.

My trees must be watered,
So their leaves will not wither.
They must be rooted and grounded
Not tossed hither and thither.

My trees must be watered,
So that everything they do will prosper.
By receiving daily the water of my Word,
My power unto them – My Gospel.

Scripture References:
Psalm 1:3, Psalm 92:13-14, Ephesians 3:14-19
Matthew 4:4, Romans 1:16

Run Your Course

Run your course
That I have planned.
It must be finished
During your time on this land.

Don't be distracted
By circumstances that arise.
Keep your focus on Me,
Don't be deceived by your eyes.

For the enemy would love
To toss you to and fro,
To get you off track
Full of worry and woe.

Don't let him succeed-
I'll fill your every need.
Speak to your storm.
Don't be filled with alarm.

For the course is worth it.
The rewards are great.
You and I determine your destiny,
There is no such thing as fate.

Scripture References:
2 Timothy 4:7, Philippians 3:13-14, Philippians 4:19
2 Corinthians 5:7, Ephesians 4:14, 26-27, Mark 11:23, Hebrews 10:35

Be Still

Be still and know
That I am God.
Have you forgotten the miracles
I performed through Moses' rod?

Don't make a choice
Between the lesser of two evils.
For I have hidden pathways
That I have yet to reveal.

Israel thought their choice
Was to drown or face the sword.
I had a pathway through the sea,
Known only by Me, the Lord.

Just because you cannot see it,
Doesn't mean it isn't there.
Don't cast away your confidence,
Cast away your care!

A fork in the road
Doesn't always limit you to left or right.
I'll make a way through the middle,
If you'll trust in My power and might.

Scripture References:
Psalm 46:10, Exodus 14:9-16, 1 Corinthians 10:13

The Treasure Is In The Temple

The treasure is in the temple,
Not way up in the sky.
It is housed in an earthen vessel,
"Abba Father" should now be your cry.

Greater is He that is within you,
Tells you where He makes His home.
You should never feel useless or worthless,
You should never feel all alone.

For I abide with My people
And dwell in them.
The two of us make a majority
Against any type of sin.

Your body is My temple,
Bought with a price.
Glorify Me in your body,
Present it to Me- a reasonable sacrifice.

Become God – Inside minded,
Instead of a distant One in the sky.
The Holy Spirit is not up here now,
He is in you, to help you through life.

Scripture References:
1 Corinthians 6:19-20, Romans 8:15, 1 John 4:4
Hebrews 13:5, 1 Corinthians 6:20

Smile My Child

Smile My child!
For yet in a little while,
You will defeat this trial,
If you go the extra mile.

Press in through prayer.
Press in through praise.
Let the authority of my Word
Rule all of your days.

There is power in purity,
So sanctify your walk.
Victory is a surety,
There will be power in your talk.

Once your life is clean,
You have authority to get mean.
You take control of the situation.
You act out the authority of My new creation.

Smile, you're only passing through.
Smile, this valley was not made for you.
Smile, this river will not overthrow you.
Smile, this fire will not even slow you.

For lo I am with you
All of your days.
Speak My Word
And Praise, Praise, Praise.

Scripture References:
Philippians 4:4, Ephesians 6:13, James 5:16, Psalms 100:4, Hebrews 4:12
Proverbs 18:21, Luke 10:19, 2 Corinthians 5:17, Psalm 23:4 Isaiah 43:2

Too Much Authority

You have too much authority
To live the way you do.
With all that authority,
Don't you believe My Word is true?

Seated with Me in the Heavenlies,
Together we rule and reign.
Far above principalities and powers,
Far above every name that is named.

For your authority to work,
First it must be known.
You can't exercise any rights
If you don't know which ones you own.

After you know it,
Now comes time to show it.
Apply what you have learned,
Until you see the situation turn.

Apply the pressure as needed,
For you will meet some resistance.
Remember, resistance causes heat on both sides,
Don't stop – maintain your persistence.

Scripture References:
Luke 10:19, Ephesians 1:21, Ephesians 2:5-6, 2 Timothy 2:15
2 Peter 1:4, Philippians 4:9

Let The Spirit Flow

Let the Spirit flow,
Don't keep Him bottled up.
Open up the door,
Running over should be your cup.

Did I not say "Out of your belly
Shall flow rivers of living water?"
This spake I of the Spirit,
Given for every son and daughter.

Every now and then
You let out a drop.
Turn the value open wide,
Let Him flow and not stop.

For a river flows with mighty force,
It is not like a small stream.
If the Spirit flows, He'll keep your life on course,
He must be the leader of your team.

As you pray in the Spirit,
The mighty rivers begin to flow.
You build yourself up on your most holy faith,
You increase your capacity to know.

You're more sensitive to the promptings.
You're more sensitive to the leadings.
When you spend time in the Word
You get revelations from the readings.

So don't hold Him in check.
Let Him flow – Let Him go.
Spend more and more time with Him.
For Him you must get to know.

Scripture References:
Psalm 23:5, John 7:38-39, Romans 8:14
John 16:13, Jude 20-21, Ephesians 1:17

Take Off The Grave Clothes

Take off the grave clothes,
For you are no longer dead.
You are risen with Me,
I took your place instead.

You were buried with Me in baptism,
The old life you did drown.
You made a statement to the world,
That you have citizenship in a new town.

Grave clothes do bind;
You are not free to live.
They must be removed,
So the new life you can live.

Even after I raised Lazarus,
He was alive and yet bound.
His grave clothes had to come off,
Allowing him freedom to get around.

The works of the flesh are grave clothes.
They try to cling to you after you're reborn.
They open doors to the enemy,
That will leave you bruised, tattered and torn.

These works must be wiped out
By the power of the Holy Spirit.
They must be replaced by fruit,
The fruit of the human spirit.

Don't think of these works
As harmless little deeds.
What you have in reality
Are deceptively powerful seeds.

Seeds that grow
And develop into roots.
Roots that penetrate deeply
And cause the growth of shoots.

Shoots then grow
And turn into trees.
Trees that can bring
Your spiritual life to its knees.

A seed of envy
Sown in your heart,
Grows into a root of bitterness
As the vicious cycle starts.

The shoot of jealousy
Is now growing in your land.
Very soon you have a tree,
The Spirit of Jealousy – A vile Strongman.

Scripture References:
Colossians 2:12, Romans 6:4, Ephesians: 2:19, John 11:43-44
Galatians 5:19-23, Acts 19:15-16, Romans 8:13
Hebrews 12:14-15, James 3:16, Numbers 5:12-15, Matthew 12:29

The Greater Road

The greater road must be traveled,
To reach your destination.
The low road will not take you there,
It was not made for the new creation.

If you travel the low road,
You will shoulder your own load.
If you travel the greater road,
You make your home in My abode.

I'll take your burden.
I'll destroy your yoke.
My Anointing will smash it,
Like the fall of a mighty oak.

The greater road separated you
From the grip of the world system.
From the hidden pitfalls of life,
You will surely learn to miss them.

Scripture References:
Matthew 10:39, Psalm 91:1, Matthew 11:28-30
Isaiah 10:27, 2 Corinthians 6:16-18

I'm Coming Again

I'm coming again;
I don't know exactly when.
I know it will be soon.
Observe the signs, seasons and the moon.

I'm coming again,
To get My glorious bride.
Without blemish, spot, or wrinkle,
A victorious church brings Me much pride.

This time when I come,
Will I find faith on the earth?
Will My bride know her rights?
Will she know what she is worth?

This time when I come,
Will you have satan underfoot?
Will you be ruling and reigning,
Walking on that crook?

The Word must be spread.
The babes must be fed.
The house must be clean.
The bride must get mean.

The job must be done.
The lost must be won.
The bride must rule and reign.
The bride must use My Name.

Scripture References:
Matthew 24:36, Matthew 28:19, Hebrews 5:13,
Luke 18:8, Ephesians 5:26-27, Romans 16:20,
Romans 5:17, Mark 16:17-18

The Edge Of Depression

You're on the edge of depression,
Don't let it pull you in.
If you allow that to happen,
You will be committing a sin.

If you give in to depression,
The enemy gets his foot in your door.
He will not settle for just his foot,
He is coming with a whole lot more.

Don't give him place.
Instead give him chase.
He is the father of lies and spirit of error,
Resist him – make him flee – make him run as if in terror.

If you give in to depression,
Then you open the door:
To the spirit of heaviness, a vile strongman,
Who will torment you even more.

Put on the oil of joy
And the garment of praise.
Arise from the weight of circumstances.
You must survive these days!

Scripture References:
Ephesians 4:27, James 4:7, John 8:44, 1 John 4:6, Isaiah 61: 1-4

In The Hands Of A Child

I have given you powerful weapons,
Nuclear in scope.
But you run around like children,
Some to the point of giving up hope.

The weapons of your warfare
Are not carnal you see.
They are mighty through Me
To set yourself free.

Free from the enemy
Who has taken you captive at his will.
Free from his devices.
Jesus paid your final bill.

Instead, you run around like children,
My mighty weapons you don't use.
When bad things happen,
You turn to me and accuse.

You have in your hands
The most powerful weapons ever known.
The Name, The Word, The Blood, The Anointing,
The Angels, The Holy Spirit – and Me on the Throne.

Don't be like a child,
Who doesn't know how to use them.
Grow into a Mighty Warrior,
When you face the enemy – <u>abuse</u> <u>him</u> !

Scripture References:
Ephesians 6:10-18, Proverbs 24:10, 2 Corinthians 10:4, 2 Timothy 2:24-26,
James 1:13, Job 38:1-2, Job 42: 1-3, Philippians 2:10
Hebrews 4:12, Revelation 12:11, Isaiah 10:27, Psalm 91
John 7: 38-39, Hebrews 12:29, Luke 10:19, Romans 16:20

The Heavenly Friends

Faith and Love
Are the heavenly friends.
They work together in your life
To achieve desired ends.

They work in harmony,
Never, ever one without the other.
Their union taps into the power of Jesus,
Our Savior and elder brother.

They have an assignment
Down here on the earth.
Their job will tell you
Just how much they are worth.

The Divine Assignment
Of the heavenly friends,
Is to eradicate from your life
The tormenting twins.

For the tormenting twins
Are Doubt and Fear.
They will rob your life
Of all God's blessing and cheer.

You must walk by faith,
But you must also walk in love.
Perfect love cast out fear,
For that does not come from above.

Walk by faith
And do not doubt.
Cast him out
With the Victory Shout!

Scripture References:
Galatians 5:16, Matthew 14:28-31 1 John 4:17-18, 2 Corinthians 5:7

Approach The Throne

In boldness and faith
Approach the throne!
For you come in Jesus' righteousness,
You don't come in your own.

For I eagerly await you
Day by day.
But so often I miss you,
For some reason you stay away.

Don't worry about your mistakes,
Repent and take care of them.
I knew you would make them,
So to the cross I sent Him.

Come! I'm not waiting to get you.
Come! I'm the one who helps you.
Come! I don't carry a stick or a whip.
Come! I'll wipe the tear from your eye.
Come! I'll wipe the frown from your lip.

For I see you through the Blood,
Not as you think you are.
I see you as holy, blameless and unreproachable,
My bright and shining star.

So hold your head high,
Be a light to the world.
Hold your head high,
Approach Me as a chosen pearl.

Scripture References:
1 Corinthians 1:30, Psalm 103:12, 1 John 1:9
Hebrews 10:19-20, Colossians 1:21-22, Psalm 119:130

Speak Life

Speak life to your affairs.
Don't dare speak your cares.
You must always speak life.
Don't give in to stress and strife.

They are there to change your words,
To speak what you see instead of your desire.
The enemy is after your words.
They give him license to drag you into the mire.

I put death and life in the power of your tongue.
Speak life over your family, especially your young.
Speak death to tragedies and diseases.
Seeing you exercise faith this way greatly pleases Me.

My Word that I have given you,
It is Spirit. It is Life.
Use it to cut through the enemy's devices
Like a well oiled knife.

Speak it loud.
Speak it clear.
When it comes out of your mouth,
It will banish fear.

Scripture References:
Mark 11:23, James 3:16, Proverbs 18:21,
Matthew 18:18, Hebrews 11:6, John 6:63

The Winds Of Change

For the winds of change
Do blow upon all.
It matters not your stature,
Whether large or small.

The winds of change do blow.
It's not like it was long ago.
Things came easy then.
All you did was sit and win.

But now you have to stand,
If you want to possess the land.
Now you have to fight,
To operate as children of light.

The enemy puts obstacles
All along your path.
You must speak them out of your way,
Let him feel your wrath.

It's not like it was before.
But don't look back with remorse.
It's not like it was before.
The violent take it by force!

Scripture References:
Ephesians 6:13-14, 1 Timothy 6:12,
Mark 11:23, Philippians 3:14, Mathew 11:12

The Power In The Oil

The power in the oil,
Is power from above.
It replaces fruitless toil,
It brings manifestation of My love.

The power in the oil,
Is due in part to its essence.
Along with My hand picked ingredients,
It also contains My presence.

The oil was a symbol
Of the Holy Spirit's power.
Today it's the anointing
Your power source in this hour.

The oil and the anointing
Represent the same thing.
The power of God in you,
To rule and reign as kings.

Not to sit back in greed,
But to help those in need.
To do the work of the Lord,
Not divided but working in one accord.

Releasing those who the enemy
Has taken captive at his will,
Setting them free to know the Lord,
Speaking into their lives "Peace Be Still."

Jesus could not do miracles,
From birth through age twenty nine.
It wasn't until He stood in the Jordan
And received from Heaven the sign.

The Holy Spirit as a dove
Anointed Him with power from on high.
From this time forward he did miracles as routine,
Yes, the Son of God, but the anointing made him mean.

He gave this anointing to us;
He left it in our trust.
It is the burden removing, yoke destroying
Power of God in us.

Scripture References:
Acts 1:8, Exodus 30:23-25, Acts 10:38, Romans 5:17, Matthew 20:26-28
Psalm 106:8-10, Mathew 3:13-17, Luke 3:21-23, Isaiah 10:27

The Season Is Here

The season is here.
Your blessings have come near.
Put away all doubt.
Bind the spirit of fear.

For things that you have planted
And things that you have sown,
Have gone through the maturation process
And now have come full grown.

It's time to harvest the crop.
Don't be moved by what you see and stop.
Claim it by faith and bring it on in.
Praise me for the victory – Sing – Sing – Sing.

Scripture References:
Matthew 18:18, 2 Timothy 1:7, Mark 4:26-32

The Dead Shall Rise

The dead shall rise
On that day of surprise,
To be caught up in the air,
From far and near.

The dead shall rise
For in Me they were asleep.
I told you it would happen;
My promises I always keep.

The dead shall rise
United with family and friends.
Death where is your sting?
You're simply a means to an end.

Scripture References:
1 Thessalonians 4:13-18

The Fire Within

I Am the ALL consuming fire.
I AM He who is the first and the last.
I AM He who has no beginning.
I Am He who burns away your past.

I Am the All consuming fire.
I burn away your sin.
I Am not some distant deity.
I Am the fire that burns within.

I change your desires
From the inside out.
Your old desire to sin
Now wants praise and shout.

The fire within burns peacefully,
When you walk in My will.
The fire turns up to check you,
When you miss Me still.

The fire roars strongly,
When sin is knocking at your door:
To keep you from sailing waters.
To keep you safely on the shore.

The fire burns brightly,
When you're in the dark of night.
It will divide wrong from right,
Confirmed by the Word to give you light.

Scripture References:
Deuteronomy 4:24, Hebrews 12:29, Psalm 37:4, Colossians 3:15
Genesis 4:7, Acts 27:9-10, Hebrews 4:12, Psalm 119:130

Don't Run From A Wounded Devil

Don't run from a wounded devil.
No believer should ever do that.
The gates of hell won't prevail against you,
But it is you, not Me, who must act.

When he tries to block your path,
Why do you try to go around him?
Don't waste time doing that,
Take your sword and crown him.

For when you use the sword against him,
You connect and deeply wound him.
Instead of finishing the job,
You take your sword and run from him.

You seek a place to hide,
Hoping he will not find you.
It won't be long before he does,
For his spirit of fear will bind you.

Stop Running! Turn and confront him!
Make him face the Armor of Light.
Your sword was made for war.
Not for running from imps of the night.

Scripture References:
Matthew 16:18, Ephesians 6:17, 2 Timothy 1:7
James 4:7, Romans 13:12, Revelation 1:16

The Feeble

The feeble must stand,
In order to possess the land.
Let the poor say I'm rich.
The weak must claim a strong hand.

To stand means to tell the devil no.
Tell him to take his junk and go.
To stand means you claim the promise,
Until it manifest you won't let go.

Stand and Speak!
Declare and Decree!
Say what you desire.
Not what you see.

Then the feeble become strong.
The sick become well.
The voice of authority triumphs.
A great testimony you can now tell.

Scripture References:
Matthew 9:6, James 4:7, 2 Peter 1:4
Mark 11:24, 2 Corinthians 5:7, Revelation 12:11

The Anointed One

I Am the anointed one.
I Am the dear Son.
I have heard you today,
As you seek Me and pray.

Stir up the anointing
Which is in you this hour.
Stir it up more often,
Then speak forth its power.

Don't keep it bottled up inside.
It must be released to coincide
With actions of faith, showing you believe,
Agreement of actions and speech ensure you receive.

Go forth releasing the anointing.
Go forth expecting to win.
Go through doors previously shut.
The anointing will let you in.

Scripture References:
Acts 10:38, Matthew 3:17, 2 Timothy 1:6
James 1:22, Act 3:5-8

The Seed Is In The Ground

The seed is in the ground.
The work has just begun.
The field must have your attention,
In order for harvest to come.

It must receive water,
By the washing of the word.
Speaking it over your seed,
Loud, so it can be heard.

The seed must have the light,
The understanding of the process.
Renew your mind to My ways
And you can work this with finesse.

The seed must be constantly weeded,
To cast down weeds of sin and doubt.
Be quick to repent-
And pull those weeds out!

The seed must grow to fullness,
Then its ready to harvest.
Put forth the sickle of mighty angels,
For as reapers, they are the best.

Scripture References:
Mark 4:3-8, Proverbs 4:20-22, Psalm 119:130
Romans 12:2, Matthew 13:22, 39, 1 John 1:9, Mark 4:28-29

Enforcers Of The Covenant

They are enforcers of My covenant,
Angelic sheriffs if you must.
My great and mighty angels,
Harkening to the spoken Word in which you trust.

They police the four corners of the earth,
Driving back the forces of hell.
They protect My people who trust Me;
They make the enemy retreat for a spell.

They are sent forth to minister
To the heirs of salvation.
They serve and protect
My precious new creation.

They are your fellow servants,
Don't give them worship that is Mine.
For in the end you will judge them,
Concerning things done in your lifetime.

Reverence the spoken Word of God.
Use it to set boundaries in your life.
Your angels will enforce them.
They protect My church, My bride, My wife.

Scripture References:
Galatians 3:19-20, Psalm 103:20, Zechariah 6:1-7
Hebrews 1:14, Revelation 19:10, 1 Corinthians 6:2-3, Psalm 138:2
Psalm 91, Hebrew 11:3

The Exodus Is Here

The Exodus is here,
For all those who draw near.
It is time to leave Egypt.
It is time to board the ship.

After you pass over
From darkness to light,
Say goodbye to all attachments
Of the hordes of the night.

At the cross of Jesus Christ
You were covered by the Blood.
If the enemy comes after you,
I will drown him in My flood.

Make your exodus from sin
And the wages it pays.
You have come into eternal life,
The blessings of God should fill your days.

The Exodus is here.
So say goodbye to fear.
Tell sickness, poverty and the second death
They can no longer come near.

The Exodus is here,
Go in and TAKE your promised land.
For if you go in and stand,
I'll back you with power from My right hand.

Scripture References:
Exodus 13:41-42, Colossians 1:13, 1 John 1:7, Revelation 12:11
Hebrews 12:1, Mark 16:20, Romans 6:23, 2 Timothy 1:7
Galatians 3:13, Matthew 11:12, Ephesians 6:13

The Neglected Armor

I have given you powerful armor,
Why do you not put it <u>all</u> on?
That's why you come out of battles
All tattered and torn.

You get excited about the shield,
And you love to wield the sword.
How dare you engage the enemy
Without the Spirit of the Lord.

The Armor does not end
In Ephesians 6:17.
Praying in the Spirit is a covering you need,
It builds your faith, makes your spirit sensitive and keen.

It's like a high powered 2 way radio,
Only your language is in code.
You can communicate with me in the throne room
Through the Holy Spirit who dwells in your abode.

Did I not say, "Out of your belly
Would flow rivers of living water?"
That is a living spiritual force,
Whose magnitude is unmatched by any other.

Scripture References:
Ephesians 6:10-18, Jude 20, 1 Corinthians 14:2, Romans 8:28
John 7:38, Hebrews 4:12

Thoughts Are Things

Thoughts are things
That the enemy brings
To control your life,
Yes, he will pull your strings.

If you entertain his thoughts,
Then you will walk his walk.
If you cast them down,
He can't lead you around.

So loose yourself from this snare.
Don't be stinking thinking unaware.
Meditate on My Word,
Not on your care.

Bring those thoughts into captivity,
Into the obedience of My Word.
Don't let them build a nest in your head,
Like an unchecked bird.

Scripture References:
Proverbs 23:7, 2 Timothy 2:26, 2 Corinthians 10:5

I Long For You

I long for you each day.
Won't you please take time to pray.
I'll give direction to your day.
Then you can be on your way.

Don't let the tyranny of the urgent
Steal our precious time.
Get with Me every day,
After all, aren't you Mine?

I have wonderful things to show you,
I have much to tell.
If you will only slow down and listen,
Then you can hear and things will go well.

I long for you each day,
To fellowship with Me.
That is why I created you,
Come praise and worship Me.

Scripture References:
Matthew 26:40, John 16:13, Matthew 6:33, 1 Corinthians 6:20
1 Corinthians 2:9-10, Ephesians 1:17,
John 10:3-4, Proverbs 1:20-33

The Way Of The World

The way of the world,
Seems right to you I know.
But I have devised a better way,
Prove Me now as we go.

The way of the world,
Says hold on to every dollar.
My way says to give,
Destroy the yoke of lack off your collar.

The way of the world,
Says borrow to get out of trouble.
My way says to give,
Then praise Me for double.

The way of the world,
Says grumble and complain when you see no way out.
My way says sing and praise Me,
Knock down Jericho's walls with a victory shout.

Scripture References:
Malachi 3:10, Proverbs 11:24, 1 Kings 17:8-16, Joshua 6:20-21

Running In Confusion

You're running in confusion,
You don't know what to do.
Pull away for a time and get with Me,
So the waves don't overtake you.

For I have set your course,
It is laid out for you to do.
But along the way are obstacles
That you must overcome too.

Don't spend all your time
Trying to get things done.
Get with Me for wisdom and direction,
And then your course will be fun.

Confusion is of the enemy;
I did not send it to you.
He's trying to thwart My plans,
But he's a liar, I'll see you through.

Get into My Word,
For its entrance will bring light,
To show you the path through confusion,
To allow you to make choices that are right.

Scripture References:
James 1:5, Jeremiah 29:11-3, Proverbs 1:20-33, Psalm 119:130
Mark 14:37, Mark 11:33, James 3:16

Jericho Must Fall

The walls of Jericho
Must come down.
They've stood long enough,
Begin to march around.

Jericho is a wall of opposition
To the will of God for you.
It must be removed,
To achieve what I called you to do.

It looks impossible I know,
But it's crumbling at the base.
Continue to praise me for the victory,
To the enemy give chase.

I knocked down Apartheid,
Communism and the Berlin Wall.
Don't you believe I can knock yours down
At your praise and victory call?

Continue to hammer away with the Word.
The gates of hell will not prevail.
It will fall to the victory shout,
And then will seem as only a fairy tale.

Scripture References:
Joshua 6:20-21, Jeremiah 23:29, Zechariah 4:7, Matthew 16:18

The Man Of Prayer

The man of prayer
Does not carry his care.
He casts it on Me,
He walks around free.

What good does it do
To come to Me and pray,
If the burden you have,
You won't let me take away?

Did I not say
The fervent prayer of the righteous availed much?
Did Jesus not make you righteous?
Is there not power in My touch?

Men ought to always pray and not faint.
Such is the lifestyle for My child – My saint.
Prayer brings Me and My power on the scene.
To work it, simply keep your lifestyle clean.

Pray with authority, expecting things to change.
It has unlimited power, it has unlimited range.
Pray in Jesus Name that your joy may be filled.
When My children are in faith, I am greatly thrilled.

Scripture References:
Psalm 55:22, 1 Peter 5:7, James 5:16
Luke 18:1, John 16:23

The Narrow Road

The road is narrow
That you must travel in life,
Not to keep you in prison,
But to keep evil out of your life.

I have designed a system
Upon which you are to live.
It doesn't agree with the world
Like My Word which says to give.

The road is narrow,
There are not many walking on it.
It takes discipline and commitment,
It is for those who are strong in spirit.

This road often takes a different course,
It doesn't go where everyone else goes.
Where it will lead to,
Sometimes only the Spirit knows.

It is hard on the flesh,
But it is designed to keep you safe.
Here, the wicked one touches you not;
Here, is your way of escape.

Scripture References:
Matthew 7:14, Matthew 20:16,
Romans 8:14, 1 John 5:18

A Work Of Grace

A work of grace has been done
Through the sacrifice of My son.
He took your place at the cross.
He paid for your gain through His loss.

He provided a way then
For you to come to Me now.
He paid ransom for your sin.
He restored you to right standing with Me now.

So don't try to approach Me
In your own estimation of goodness.
Come by the way He made,
By the Blood of Jesus and His righteousness.

Then you will not measure yourself
By what you have or have not done.
You will then fully realize
Your privileges as a Blood washed son.

Then you will enter in
With confidence and boldness.
Then you will partake of Me
In the beauty of holiness.

Scripture References:
Matthew 20:28, Hebrews 4:16, Hebrews 10:19

Dwelling In The Fire

Yes, my child,
You can dwell in the fire.
For you are clothed with the Lord Jesus,
Righteousness and Priestly attire.

My fire will hot harm you,
It may make your face shine.
That's what happened to Moses and Jesus,
They touched that glory of Mine.

It's an oven to the wicked,
Burning them up like stubble.
It's a warm fire to the righteous,
Bringing healing and light in times of trouble.

You can dwell in the fire,
Your hands are clean and hearts pure.
It is My manifested presence,
For those who are Blood washed and sure.

Don't be afraid of the fire,
It only consumes sin.
Desire My manifested presence,
I want to talk to you – <u>Come</u> <u>On</u> <u>In</u> !

Scripture References:
Psalm 15:1-5, Matthew 17: 1-3, Malachi 4:1-2
Psalm 24:3-4, Deuteronomy 4:24

The Mountain

For I say unto you this day,
You have taken time to pray.
I will surely make a way,
Cast your cares on Me today.

The battle is Mine;
The victory is yours.
This was put in your path
To get you off course.

Use My Word,
And use My Name.
Call it null and void,
And I'll render it the same.

Don't back down from mountains,
You will face many in your life.
Speak to them – they will be removed.
Get in agreement – you and your wife.

Scripture References:
1 Peter 5:7, Matthew 18:19-20
Isaiah 54:17, Philippians 2:9-10

Mountains Shall Be Moved

Mountains shall be moved,
When you apply the force of faith.
They shall be cast into the sea,
When you doubt not, but believe.

If you had faith as a seed,
Then you would say:
"Mountain, in the Name of Jesus,
You must get out of my way."

Part of saying is sowing,
Part of saying is growing.
Eventually, the faith seed is full grown,
Then, you will see the mountain going.

The process is working all the time.
Don't give up in the early stages;
Stay with it 'till circumstances come in line,
To your testimony add victory pages.

Scripture References:
Mark 11:23, Matthew 17:20, Mark 4:28

Agree With Me

Oh that My children
Would agree with Me.
Then they would learn
How to live totally free.

I say one thing,
The world says another.
Why don't you listen
To the words of your elder brother?

The power of agreement
Is a magnifying force.
It multiples your faith;
It gives you the victory to stay on course.

If you agree with Me,
Then think My thoughts.
Don't clutter your mind
With all the junk the enemy brought.

Then you will be single minded,
Not tossed to and fro.
Then, you will receive from Me,
What you've asked for plus a whole lot more.

If you agree with Me,
Then say what I say.
My words framed the worlds,
Let them frame yours each day.

Speak forth the desires
That I have placed in your heart.
Don't look back at the past,
Agree with Me for a new start.

Call those things into manifestation
That I have given you in My Word.
Hearing you calling and using the Name,
Is one of the sweetest sounds I've ever heard.

So think like Me and talk like Me,
Create for yourself a better life.
But beware; the enemy will come after you,
With his number one weapon – **<u>STRIFE</u>** !

Scripture References:
Proverbs 8:34, Isaiah 55:8-9, Hebrews 11:3 Psalm 37:4,
Philippians 3:13-14, Romans 4:17
3 John 1:3-4, James 3:16

In My Name

I have given you the Name
Of unlimited power.
The righteous run into it,
It is a strong tower.

I told you to ask the Father,
In My Name.
Your joy should be full,
Your life should never be the same.

In My Name,
And faith in My Name,
Blind eyes see
And up walk the lame.

In My Name,
Demons are subject.
Your name is in the Book,
Separating you from the general public.

In My Name,
Every knee must bow.
Those in Heaven, those on earth,
And under the earth NOW !

Don't take My Name for granted,
Don't ever take it in vain.
I gave it to you for a reason,
To control the evil one – he is **<u>INSANE</u>** !

Scripture References:
Mark 16:17-18, Philippians 2:10, Luke 10:17, Acts 3:6-7 John 16:23-24, Proverbs 18:10

Do What You Love

Do what you love
For your desires come from above.
I have placed them there;
They are entrusted to your care.

Did I not say that I would give you
The desires of your heart?
Child, I put them there.
Go ahead, make your start.

When you do what you love
Your gifts and talents begin to show.
You find your purpose in life,
Then your anointing begins to grow.

You find the peace that you long for-
The fulfillment that you crave.
You become one with your Creator.
Your gifts don't go unused to the grave.

There is unlimited achievement
When you line up with My will.
Take time to come into My presence.
Take time to get quiet and be still.

Scripture References:
Psalm 37:4, Romans 11:29, 1 Timothy 4:14, 2 Timothy 1:6
Proverbs 18:16, Mathew 25:21, 2 Peter 1:10

Work The WORD

There are many who ask:
Does the Word really work?
To these I ask:
Do you put the Word to work?

You must Work The Word !
Practice what you have learned and heard.
The blessings come to those
Who are doers of the Word.

Don't ask the question:
Will the Word work for me?
Use it like a tool,
Set yourself free.

A tool you inquire?
Yes – Did I not say-
My Word was a hammer, a river,
A sword, a seed, a rock, and an all consuming fire?

The Word works only
To the degree that you use it.
When evil comes
Why do you not always choose it?

You run to this,
You run to that,
The word sits neglected
Like a forgotten old hat.

Work The Word !
It will work for you.
It is mighty in battle,
It is tried, tested, and true.

Scripture References:
Philippians 4:9, James 1:22-25, Jeremiah 23:29, Hebrews 4:12, Luke 8:11, Psalm 18:30

Prove Me Now

Prove me now
Thus saith the Lord,
If I'll not open the windows of the Heaven
Just on your accord.

Be faithful to tithe;
Be faithful to give.
These two principles have much to do
With the way you move and live.

Enforce the rebuke
I put on the devourer.
Bind him in Jesus Name.
Stand! Don't be a cowerer.

You have deposited much
Into your Heavenly account.
Much fruit has abounded,
Make withdrawals – you determine the amount.

Call it forth in Jesus Name.
Praise me for it daily.
Prove me now saith God,
If I will not give to you faithfully.

Scripture References:
Malachi 3:10-12, Matthew 18:18, Romans 4:17

There Comes A Time

There comes a time
When you must decide.
If you will follow Me
Or take the way that is wide.

For narrow is My way
And there is a price you must pay.
Will you live by what you feel,
Or will you live by what I say?

Though it may hurt at first,
It will turn out all right.
Did I not say I have plans for you?
I have greater things in sight.

Don't live by the flesh
Or the unrenewed mind.
Meditate My Word-
Become a being of superior kind.

Your soul gets stronger
The more your flesh is denied.
Your faith gets stronger
The more the Word is applied.

Make a decision
On how you will live.
Your feelings will follow,
Control of your life – to them you must <u>not</u> give.

Scripture References:
Matthew 7:14, Matthew 4:4, Jeremiah 29:11, Galatians 5:6
2 Corinthians 5:17, Ephesians 3:16, Romans 10:17

I'm A Winner

I am a winner.
I will not fail.
The Greater One dwells within me,
He puts me over- I will prevail.

For since the Lord God is for me,
Doesn't matter who is against me.
Jesus and I are a majority-
Every foe must flee.

I have the mind of Christ,
Renewed to His Word.
I take heed to what I hear,
I don't believe everything I've heard.

My body is the temple
Of the mighty Holy Spirit.
With a guest like this,
I don't allow sin and sickness to come near it.

My spirit is in contact
With my great and mighty God.
I perform miracles as routine,
Like in the days of Moses' rod.

Scripture References:
2 Corinthians 2:14, Mark 4:24
1 Corinthians 6:19-20

Deliverance Comes

For deliverance comes
On the wings of faith,
To protect you, to hold you up
To keep you safe.

I said I'll never leave you.
I said I'll never forsake you.
There is no situation on this earth
From which My right hand cannot take you.

Trust in Me,
With My Word agree.
Submit to Me.
The enemy must flee.

Hold your head up.
Expect to be delivered.
I'll show myself strong.
Be brave – don't quiver.

Scripture References:
Hebrews 13: 5-6, James 4:7

I AM With You!

Lo! For this I would say
To you this day.
Do not fret…Do not worry
If you can't see your way.

I have helped you in the past,
So your confidence please don't cast.
I'm here with you now,
I'll teach you how,

To hear from me
When you come to pray
To hear from me
As you go your way.

For I'll not leave you helpless.
I'll not leave you alone.
I still run this earth.
I'm still on the throne.

I have great things planned
For you to do.
You can't stop now
And say you're through.

You must get beyond this,
It's a mountain looming large.
Use the authority I gave you,
Use it to take charge.

For I back that authority,
I make sure it comes to pass.
There's a mountain in front of you now,
And it won't be your last.

Scripture References:
Matthew 28:20, 1 Peter 5:7, Hebrews 10:35, Hebrews: 5-6

You're Special To Me, Child

You're special to Me child.
Come rest with Me a while.
You're weary from the battle,
Come refresh yourself with My mantle.

You've traveled many places,
Some were not in My plan for you.
Use My presence as an oasis,
Get refreshed, get built up, and get renewed.

You're special to Me child.
Stay and rest with Me awhile.
Now is not the time to make an election,
Stay in my presence and receive direction.

The warfare is intense.
The battle rages on.
Shore up your defense.
Sing your victory song.

You're special to Me child.
Fulfill the plan I have for you.
You're special to Me child.
You will enjoy what I have for you to do.

Scripture References:
Matthew 11:28-29, Jeremiah 29:11, Jeremiah 33:3

Power On Demand

You have power on demand,
To help you walk through this land.
It is resident in Me,
But it must be tapped into by thee.

Remember the lady,
With the issue of blood?
She tapped into My power,
And it came out like a flood.

I didn't initiate that power,
It flowed because of her faith.
Her faith touched Me in that hour,
It made her healed, whole, and safe.

Remember the lame man,
Lying at the gate,
Day after day crying for help,
Day after day having to wait?

Peter and John came by one day,
They perceived he had faith to be healed.
They used My Name – demanded My power,
Immediately his crippling sentence was repealed.

Make a demand on My power,
And use My mighty Name.
You too will heal the sick,
You too will raise the lame.

Scripture References:
John 14: 13-14 Matthew 9:20-22
Acts 3:1-8, Mark 16:15-19

Vessels Of Honor

You must be a vessel of honor,
To accomplish My work on the earth.
You must believe in yourself,
You must realize what you're worth.

For some are vessels of clay,
For some are vessels of wood.
Don't be satisfied in this condition,
Rise to the next level – really you should.

I am no respecter of persons,
I don't make one vessel good and one bad.
It is up to you to choose,
Which vessel you'll be - my lad.

Become a vessel of honor,
Become a vessel of gold.
Leave old things in the past,
Cleanse yourself – Be Bold!

Scripture References:
2 Timothy 2:19-21

Protect Your Head

Protect your head at all cost,
Don't even start to think like the lost.
I have given you My Word,
Don't let thoughts land like a nesting bird.

Renew your mind.
Protect your head.
Instead of the hat of worry,
Don the Helmet of Salvation instead.

Bring every thought captive,
To the obedience of Christ.
Don't let your mind wander,
Don't treat it so nice.

Take those thoughts captive,
Take them by force.
Renew your mind to the Word,
Get it back on the right course.

Protect your head!
For actions are conceived in the mind.
Meditate the Word – Act on the Word,
Keep your Helmet on **ALL** the time.

Scripture References:
Ephesians 6:17, 2 Corinthians 10:3-5, Proverbs 23:7
Philippians 4:8, Romans 12:2, James 1:22

Waves Of Glory

I am coming to visit you,
Riding on waves of glory.
Your testimony will be awesome.
You will bless others when you tell the story.

For My glory shall overshadow you,
You will be kept by the power of the Most High.
You will be shielded and protected,
Evil will not be able to come nigh.

When My glory comes near,
It banishes doubt, unbelief and fear.
You will not be able to stand,
You will be on your face, my man.

When you get up,
You will not be the same.
You will be a changed man.
You will have boldness to claim-

The benefits of salvation
That are yours for the taking-
Were bought and paid for at the cross.
His resurrection left Hell quaking.

As I ride in on waves of glory,
I will have much to say of your life story.
I will give you direction about your future.
I'll sew up your wounds like a surgeon with a suture.

Scripture References:
John 11: 38-44, Luke 4:18-19, 1 Corinthians 2:6-10, Psalms 91:1
1 Peter 1:3-5, 2 Corinthians 3:7-18, Colossians 2:11-15

Hear Me My Child

Hear Me My child,
Come rest with Me awhile.
The battle has made you weary;
Even of Me you are now leary.

You have become skeptical
Of spiritual things.
You are entertaining unbelief,
You are straying from the King of Kings.

You are moved by what you see.
You are losing your trust in me.
You are believing what you see-
Not what you have heard from Me.

Enter into My rest,
So you can receive My best.
Don't carry this thing in your chest-
Rest in Me and be blessed.

Scripture References:
Matthew 11:28, Hebrews – Chapter 3

Wake Up And Live

Wake up and live,
You have too much to give.
Don't sit around feeling sorry,
Start working on your tomorrow.

There is much to be done.
Grow into the image of My Son.
Study His life and ways,
Model Him and improve your days.

Arise and thresh!
Beat those mountains low.
Thresh them to pieces,
They'll vanish in the wind My Spirit blows.

Get up and go!
You already know
A small part of the plan,
So do what you can.

Study the Word of truth,
Become a workman in its use.
Develop yourself through its exercise,
Become highly skilled in its use.

Scripture References:
Micah 4:13, 2 Timothy 2:15, Isaiah 41:14-16

The Ancient of Days

I am the Ancient of Days,
You must come to know My ways.
You are familiar with My acts.
You have studied them in the facts.

In order to know My ways,
You must spend time with Me.
Come in to the banquet table,
It cost you nothing, it's free.

For I long for My people,
To come and sup with Me.
All is waiting and prepared,
Allow the Father and Me to abide in thee.

I created you for fellowship,
For abiding with Me.
Pull away from the busyness,
Get My perspective, then you can see.

Scripture References:
Daniel 7:9, Psalms 103:7, Revelation 3:20
Hebrews 11:6, John 15:1-7

Ritual and No Substance

You have ritual and no substance.
Your efforts are vain and wasted.
Come deeper into My Presence,
A drink from Me you should have tasted.

Don't do things like a robot
Blindly going through the motions.
Give serious thought to what you do,
You should have a return on your devotions.

If you're going to pray,
Also take the time to hear.
One of the reasons for praying,
Is to get My direction for you clear.

Don't feel good,
Just because you prayed for an hour.
Feel good and be built up
Because you have experienced My power.

Let your time with Me count for something.
It should be life changing in scope.
Don't just punch a time clock with Me,
Let me lead you and give you hope.

Scripture References:
Matthew 6:17-18, 2 Timothy 3:5,
John 4:14, John 10:2-4, Ephesians 3:16-19

He's Waiting On The Word

He's waiting on the Word!
So let your voice be heard.
Speak forth the promises of God,
See miracles like from Moses' rod.

In the beginning,
He hovered over the deep.
What was He waiting for?
The Word of God to speak.

He was the power source at creation,
Just waiting for the spoken word.
He is your power source today,
He is waiting to see what you will say.

Will you speak forth the Word?
Or will you say what you've seen and heard?
Will you speak forth your desire?
Or will you say what's got you in the mire?

Will you give Him the Word,
And watch Him perform His work?
Or will you grumble and murmur,
And act like a worldly jerk?

Jesus always gave Him the Word,
And He always went to work.
Confirming it with signs and wonders,
Manifesting Himself without quirk.

That same Spirit of God,
Now dwelleth in us.
Will you give Him the Word,
So you can learn to trust?

He's waiting for the Word,
That Great and Holy One.
Give it to Him now,
Stand back and watch the fun.

Scripture References:
Genesis 1:1-11, Acts 1:8, Romans 8:11

Seek My Face

Because you seek My face,
You will find extra mercy and grace.
You will find help in time of trouble
I'll not delay – I'll be there on the double.

I said these who seek Me early find Me.
You have sought – Here I am.
I'll never leave you nor forsake you
Lo, I am with you – I, the Lamb.

I will guide you by My Spirit.
By the inward witness I'll do it.
Don't look for guidance out there.
Look within, where the Spirit is so near.

Don't listen with your outward ears,
You'll not hear Me with those.
That's not the way I planned it.
That's not the way I chose.

Become attuned to the voice of the Spirit,
Train yourself constantly in this area.
The Spirit, He dwelleth within,
Oh, He is so near to you.

Continue to seek Me,
Listening daily at My gates.
When you find Me, you'll find life,
You'll find favor and grace.

Scripture References:
Romans 8:11, 1 Chronicles 16:11, 2 Chronicles 7:14,
Hebrews 11:6, Romans 8:14

Stay Close To Me

Though an host should encamp against thee,
Thou shalt not fear.
Lo, I am not far away,
I am always near.

I am He who walks with you,
I am He who plans your course.
I am He who looks after you,
I am He who guides you safely to the shores.

Do not stray away from Me,
Talk to Me daily.
I'll keep you through the problems.
I'll keep you from failing.

Stay close to Me in prayer,
Stay close to Me in the Word.
Don't stray from the nest,
Like a maverick bird.

Your strength is in prayer,
And also in the Word.
Seek My face always,
Through praise, let your voice be heard.

Scripture References:
Isaiah 43:5, Psalm 27:3, James 4:8

You Need An Hour of Power

You need an hour of power,
To always start your day.
Don't ever dash out unprepared,
And go out naked into the fray.

Take time for your whole armor,
Be spiritually dressed when you go out.
Then when the fiery darts come,
They'll hit your shield and be put out.

Get with Me for your orders,
Then you'll avoid much conflict.
You'll fight the ones concerning your borders,
The unnecessary one you won't pick.

Come into My presence,
My anointing will smear you-
With yoke destroying power,
Demons will tremble and fear you.

Build yourself up,
On your most holy faith.
Praying in the Spirit with Holy Ghost Power
To keep you charged up, sensitive, and safe.

Take time for worship.
Take time for praise.
I will inhabit your praise,
And ordain strength for your days.

Meditate on the Name,
It gives you power to claim,
Authority in three worlds.
It'll bring you all of Heaven's pearls.

Scripture References:
Mark 14:34:37, Isaiah 10:27, Psalm 22:3,
Jude 20, Philippians 2:10-12

Stop Chasing The Wind

Stop chasing the wind,
<u>Get</u> <u>a</u> <u>grip</u>! My friend.
You're running here and there,
Tossed to and fro with every care.

Slow down and focus
On what I've called you to do.
Put your tool in one hand,
In the other, wield the sword I've given you.

Be focused, be fruitful and finish
The tasks you have at hand.
Work like Nehemiah,
Focused, discerning, doing My will in the land.

Be wise to the enemy's interruptions,
For they are meant to distract you.
Keep yourself pure – allow no corruption,
You will still be standing when the attacks are through.

So get on with the work,
With the tool and the sword.
You have all of Heaven behind you,
Yes, even Me, the Lord!

Scripture References:
Ephesians 4:14-15, Ephesians 4:24-27, Matthew 10:16
Mathew 11:28-30, 2 Peter 1:10, Nehemiah 4:17

Songs Of Deliverance

For songs of deliverance
Shall be sung by you tonight.
For you have finally reached the point,
Where you now give up this fight.

The battle is not yours
But Mine saith the Lord.
Sing songs of deliverance,
Sing songs from My Word.

Scripture References:
2 Chronicles 20:14-17 Psalm 32: 6-7

The Prevailing Wind

The wind of My Spirit,
Is a prevailing wind.
It blows away iniquity.
It blows away sin.

It is all over the earth
Hovering just like in the beginning.
It is waiting for you to speak
"Grace!" to your mountain and start winning.

For I have created in you,
A sharp threshing instrument with teeth.
Thresh those mountains into powder,
To be blown into the sea.

Scripture References:
Genesis 1: 1-3, Zechariah 4:6-7, Isaiah 41:15-16

The Sun of Righteousness

The Sun of Righteousness has come
With Healing in His wings.
Restoration and wholeness
Are also gifts He brings.

I bring these to My people,
Who have humbled themselves to seek Me.
I bring them to these people,
So that they will be set free.

For you have turned from your way,
To seek Me today.
I have heard from Heaven,
I have heard you pray.

Now, I will heal your land,
I will give you My plan.
You have sought My face,
You have found My grace.

Scripture References:
Malachi 4:1-3, 2 Chronicles 7:14

The Taming of the Tongue

The taming of the tongue
Is very difficult for the young.
They say everything they see and feel,
They don't realize they're making a deal.

For words set the boundaries
And frame your very life.
Words bring peace and joy
Or they bring conflict and strife.

Whatever you say you strengthen,
Bad situations you can even lengthen,
By saying what you see
Instead of what the Word says it should be.

By your words you are justified,
By your words you are condemned.
Why would you speak against the Word
When you know it comes from him?

The tongue no man can tame,
That's why I gave you the Holy Spirit.
That's the first thing He takes control of,
With His power you no longer fear it.

I put life and death in the power of your tongue
And you won't even take time to tame it.
If it's building your world day by day,
Shouldn't YOU be the one to frame it?

Scripture References:
James 3: 5-9, Hebrews 11:3, Matthew 12:37
Proverbs 18:21, Mark 11:23

I Came To Set The Captive Free

I came to set the captive free,
But you My friend,
Must walk out that liberty.
I've done all that I can do,
The rest is now squarely up to you.

I went to the cross
To purchase your freedom.
I redeemed your life
And put you in a new Kingdom.

Your spirit man is free,
So your mind and body must be.
Renew your mind to My Word,
Present your body to Me.

You have to think free,
Before you can be free,
Then you will talk free,
And that My friend is the key.

You must be renewed
In the spirit of your mind.
Think like a new species
That never existed before in time.

Think like one
Who has the mind of Christ.
After all, you do,
It was bought with a price.

See yourself free!
See yourself released!
As a man thinketh in his heart,
So he will be.

Speak forth your deliverance,
Declare that you are free!
For in order to receive victory,
Heaven and Earth must agree!

Scripture References:
Luke 4:18-20, Romans 12:1-2, Ephesians 4:20-24

The Anointing Within

The Anointing within
Is where deliverance begins.
But it must be released,
To see your storm cease.

Greater is He that is within you
Than he that is in the world.
Release Him to work on your behalf,
He is Heaven's great and priceless pearl.

Christ in you
Is your hope of glory.
Unleash Him now to work for you,
Then to others tell your story.

He whom God has sent,
Has the Spirit without measure.
Yes, you are an earthen vessel,
But keep your eyes on the inward treasure.

Burdens will be removed,
Yokes will be destroyed.
Mountains will fall into the sea,
When this power of God is deployed.

Scripture References:
Colossians 1:25-27, John 3:34, Isaiah 10:27,
1 John 2:27-28

Stir Up The Gift That Is Within You

Stir up the gift that is within thee,
I put it there for a reason.
It is not for occasional use,
It is not just for a season.

It is there to minister life,
To other members of My Body.
It is there to serve others,
Serve in Excellence! Don't be shoddy.

Gifts lie dormant within,
They must be stirred up.
You stir them up through using them,
To running over will I fill your cup.

The more you use them,
The sharper they become.
Be faithful over little,
And a Greater Anointing will come.

Scripture References:
Hebrews 5:14, 1 Timothy 4:14, 2 Timothy 1:6
Romans 11:29, Luke 19:15-17

You Can't Go Down

You can't go down,
I need you to stand.
I'll stand with you,
Together, we'll take the land.

You can't go down,
If you're standing on the Word.
It's not going anywhere,
This, you've already heard.

You can't go down,
In fact, you can go up.
Come up into My presence,
Together we will sup.

Come up and sit with Me
In Heavenly places.
You'll see things differently then,
If this were cards,
We would hold <u>all</u> <u>the</u> <u>aces</u>.

Rise up and stand!
I know you can!
Don't just exist.
Flourish and accomplish.

I am the Vine,
You are the branch.
Don't just believe for a room,
You can own the whole ranch.

Release your faith,
Then praise it on in.
I did not create you to lose,
I made you to <u>Win</u>! <u>Win</u>! <u>Win</u>!

Scripture References:
Ephesians 2:4-7, John 10:10
Ephesians 6:13-18, John 15:5-8

Expecting To Receive – 1

You must be <u>expecting</u> to receive
That for which you have prayed and believed.
You must remain single minded,
To manifest what you have conceived.

You must <u>say</u> only what you expect,
Not what you may see.
You will have what you say
Not what already may be.

You must <u>think</u> on what you desire,
Not on the way it already is.
You are baptized with the Holy Spirit and Fire.
You exchange your creativity for His.

You must <u>see</u> only your request,
Visualize it night and day.
I always send My best,
Receive It! – After all, you <u>did</u> pray.

You must <u>act</u> like you have it,
So thank Me in advance.
Prayer is also part of your armor,
In verse 18 – the long distance Lance!

Scripture References:
Acts 3:1-5, Philippians 4:8, Proverbs 4:20-27 Mark 11:23-24, Ephesians 6:18

There's A Miracle In Your Mouth

There's a miracle in your mouth.
Don't let circumstances keep heading south.
Put a stop to them now–
Open your mouth – you know how.

Issue a cease and desist!
Come on, you can have your wish.
For the Name will bring a halt,
To all forces currently on assault.

Don't put up with the frogs another day,
Command them be on their merry way.
You have places to go and things to do.
Don't let another day go by
In which they hinder you.

With the Name command evil to go,
With the Name command blessings to come.
The Name will work for all My children,
It is not restricted to only some.

You control your miracle,
With what you believe and say.
Speak it into existence <u>NOW</u> !
Don't wait for some distant day.

Scripture References:
Exodus 8:1-10, Mark 11:23, Proverbs 18:21, Matthew
12:37, Philippians 2:10, Galatians 3:5

Praise Is The Reel

Praise is the reel-
That brings in your catch.
To the doorway of blessings,
It's the finger that opens the latch.

Once you have named it,
And you have claimed it,
You better praise it on in,
If you want to frame it.

Praise creates a pathway
For Me to move on your behalf.
Praise your way to victory,
In the end, you and I will laugh.

Praise Says: "Thank You Lord – It's already done."
I Say: "Here it is child – Go have some fun."

Scripture References:
Psalm 22:3, Isaiah 53: 10-12
Psalm 8:2, Matthew 21:16

A Picture of Praise

There is a picture of praise
In My Word for you to see.
It is a proven technique,
A sure path to victory.

It is the story of Israel
At war against the enemy.
The battle was fierce,
It raged on relentlessly.

Then Moses stood up high,
For all Joshua's warriors to see.
He lifted holy hands to the sky,
His arms formed a V-for Victory,

As long as he lifted holy hands,
The armies of Israel prevailed.
When his arms grew weary
And fell to his side,
The enemy got stronger,
The battle changed its tide.

Then Moses got some help,
Intercessors if you wish.
They held him up before the Lord,
Assuring that victory would be accomplished.

For you see, I inhabit your praise,
I enthrone Myself there.
If you could see into the spirit realm,
You would see Angels everywhere.

They would finish the battle,
In the Heavenly sphere.
Then you would see the manifestation of it,
Where you are down there.

Scripture References:
Revelation 12:7-11, Exodus 17: 10-12, Psalm 22:3

The Limiting Factor

There is a limiting factor,
That restrains My work on the earth.
It is a people who don't know who they are,
They don't know what in Christ they're worth.

They operate mainly on hope,
They hardly walk in faith.
They stay mainly on the shores,
Where it's comfortable, secure and safe.

I have given them My entire Word,
And the universal Authority of My Name.
I have given them the Spirit without measure,
Just like Me and My Disciples – The Same!

Yet, they believe Me for crumbs,
When they could have the banquet table.
They don't know Me at all,
They don't know - <u>I AM Able!</u>

Don't limit Me with your unbelief.
Don't have such a tiny vision.
Choose to believe in Me and My Word.
Don't go by your feelings – make a decision!

Scripture References:
John 3:34, John 17:18, John 20:21-23
Matthew 13: 54-58

Justified By Thy Words

By thy words thou art justified.
By thy words thou art condemned.
Everything that happens in life,
Cannot be blamed on him.

For he is a deceiver and liar,
Been that way from the beginning.
Don't let him use your own mouth,
To cause you to keep on sinning.

For he and his hosts,
Are the birds of the air.
They come to steal the Word,
And fill you with care.

They bombard your thoughts night and day,
They are relentless in their attack.
They hope to control your words,
To keep you lost, sick, and in lack.

They know that what you think,
You will eventually say.
If they control your thoughts,
Then they control your way.

Don't dare say what they say!
Don't enter into agreement with him.
If you do, you sign for his package,
And your life will be condemned.

Say what the Word says,
For it is tested and tried.
This is submitting to God and resisting him,
He will flee and you'll be justified.

Scripture References:
Matthew 12:37, John 8:44
Mark 4:4, 13-15, James 4:7

Arise

Arise My child,
And take thy place.
Lay aside every sin and weight,
And run thy race.

Arise from the prostration
That circumstances have kept you.
Remember, you're seated with Me
In Heavenly places.
Circumstances are under your feet-
They look up to you.

Walk on them with the Authority of My Name,
Stand on them and the promises you claim.
Yea, they might bruise your heel,
But, you'll bruise their head – for real!

Arise! My child, don't lie down.
Arise! Together we wear the victor's crown.
Arise! Your armor is useless in a prone position.
Arise! You have to be walking for the Great Commission.

Come back to the water,
Come back to the wine.
Come into My presence and get refreshed,
Then go back to the battle-
Standing this time!

Scripture References:
Joshua 1:2, Ephesians 2:6, Luke 10:19 Genesis 3:15, Ephesians 6:13

Receive From Me

Receive from Me!
Receive from Me!
It is not hard you see
To receive from Me.

You must position yourself,
That's the first step to do.
Body, soul, and spirit all must agree
That what you have asked will come through.

Your spirit's already lined up,
And in agreement with Me.
It is your soul and body
That must be loosed and set free.

With your soul you must think
Like you have received already.
Set your will and control your emotions,
Keep them lined up and steady.

With your body you must act
Like it's already done.
Lifting holy hands to praise and thank Me
The victory is already won.

Scripture References:
Acts 3:5, Romans 12:2, 1 Timothy 2:8

The Walls Must Come Down

The walls must come down
From around your Jericho town.
You must knock them to the ground-
Then they will no longer have you bound.

They are walls of containment,
Designed to keep your life squeezed.
You knock them down by singing,
Shouting and praising on your knees.

The walls cannot stand against you,
They have a weakness in their ranks.
Their gates will not prevail against you,
So praise Me and give Me thanks.

So march with a victory song,
Then it will not be long.
The walls will come down,
You will wear the victor's crown.

Scripture References:
Joshua 6:20, Matthew 16:18

The Spoken Word

It is through the spoken Word of God
That your faith comes.
It comes by hearing Me speak to you,
Audibly, inwardly or quickened the logos becomes.

This is what you live by-
Not just bread alone!
Every spoken Word proceeding from Me,
Coming directly from My throne.

It is a personal, customized sword,
Designed for you and your situation.
I do not leave you helpless,
I take care of My new creation.

For the Sword of the Spirit,
Is My spoken Word to man.
That's why in the Revelation,
It's in My mouth – not My hand.

For I uphold all things
By the spoken Word of My power,
The worlds were framed by My spoken Word,
Back in the beginning hour.

When I give you a Word – Use It-
Both on the enemy and your own mind!
That's why I told Timothy to wage warfare,
With the prophecies I spoke to him in his time.

The spoken Word is Dangerous!
It is a sharp Two Edged Sword.
It got one edge when it came from My mouth,
It gets the other when it comes out of yours.

For the Sword of the Spirit,
Is quick and powerful you see.
It was honed and shaped
And designed by Me.

Scripture References:
Romans 10:17, Ephesians 6:17, Hebrews 1:3
Matthew 4:4, Revelation 19:15, 21, Hebrews 11:3

Access To My Throne

You have access to My throne!
You have access to My throne!
You don't need one to come for you;
You come directly on your own.

I made a way through the Blood
For you to come to the throne.
Don't come with fear and doubt,
Come in faith on your own.

You are coming to the throne of grace,
Not the throne of judgment.
Put a smile on you face,
Have a look of contentment.

I said you would find help
In the time of need.
So come expecting to receive
As your case you do plead.

For I see you through the Blood,
Not as you see yourself.
Holy, blameless and unreproachable,
A giant warrior – not a christian elf.

Scripture References:
Hebrews 4:16, Hebrews 9:6-15

Suddenly!

Suddenly! In a moment,
In the twinkling of an eye,
I will manifest Myself to you,
Like the falling star across the sky.

When you least expect it,
I'll be there.
Standing beside you,
Just because I care.

Suddenly! In an instant,
I'll show up in your affairs,
To straighten things out,
To silence your cares.

Suddenly! In a moment,
You'll wonder where it all went.
The mountains that loomed before you,
Like old garments will now be rent.

Suddenly! In a day,
It will all be in place.
That for which you have prayed,
Now continue to run your race.

Scripture References:
Isaiah 48:3, Malachi 3:1

The Fish Are In The Sea

The fish are in the sea,
The fish are in the sea.
They are not on the land,
Go cast your nets for Me.

They are not in the church.
They are not in the mountains.
They are not in the valley.
They are not in the desert.

I find My people everywhere
But where the fish are.
How can you fish for Me,
When from the fish you are too far?

Go where the fish are,
Then let down your nets.
I'll help you bring them in,
I'll help you with your catch.

Scripture References:
Matthew 4:19-20, Matthew 28:18-20, Acts 1:8

Let The River Flow

Let the river flow,
Let it flow up to Me.
Your praise is a delight,
A delight you cannot see.

Praise Me with your understanding,
Praise Me in the Spirit.
It's praise either way,
The enemy will not come near it.

It comes out of your belly,
Like rivers of living water.
This is the day of prophecy,
For all My sons and daughters.

Let the river flow,
Let it ascend to Me.
I will inhabit your praise,
The enemy will turn and flee.

Let the river flow,
I'll make strong these who are weak.
Let the river flow,
Then listen as I speak.

Scripture References:
1 Corinthians 14:15, John 7:38, Psalm 22:3

Fear <u>NOT</u>!

Why do you fear,
When you know I am near?
I'll never leave you nor forsake you,
I'll never let anything take you.

The spirit of fear is not from Me.
Don't receive anything I didn't send to thee.
That kind of spirit will manifest in your mind,
Creating disastrous imaginations
Of an ungodly kind.

Once you've been born again,
Fear no longer comes from within.
It comes mainly from what you hear and see,
An external evil designed to torment thee.

Deal with it,
Like the devil himself.
It's a pesky little spirit,
An irritating elf.

Submit yourself to Me,
Resist it with the Name and the Word.
It will flee from you,
Like a wounded bird.

Walk with Me
And walk in faith.
I am with you,
I'll keep you safe.

Scripture References:
Isaiah 41:10, James 4:7, 2 Timothy 1:7, Romans 8:15

The Weapons

Why do you stare at his weapons?
Why do you gaze at them in awe?
I told you they would not prosper;
I told you they would not go far.

Yet, you take My weapons
And you always lay them down,
And marvel at the situations
The enemy has placed all around.

I told you that My weapons
Were mighty through Me.
Be moved by what I say,
Not by what you see.

My weapons are the **most powerful**,
But also the least used.
Instead of standing and fighting,
My people turn to Me and accuse.

Stop Blaming Me! - I'm on your side!
Let's get together and agree.
Let's turn the battle tide.
Let's make the enemy flee.

Pick up My weapons and use them,
They are designed by Me to win.
I stand behind every one of them,
I AM your Lord, you Savior, your Friend.

Scripture References:
Ephesians 6:10-18, 2 Corinthians 10:3-4, 2 Corinthians 5:7
Isaiah 54:17

Taking Care Of Business

You take care of My business,
I'll take care of yours.
Your priorities are out of line,
You're doing all the wrong chores.

You are striving in the flesh,
Trying to fix your own mess.
Get in My presence and get refreshed,
Come on in – be My guest.

Then you will find
True peace of mind.
Things will work out
All of the time.

Scripture References:
Matthew 6:33, Psalm 16:11, Psalm 22:3-4
Zechariah 4:6, Haggai 1:2-8

Draw Nigh Unto Me

Draw nigh unto Me!
Draw nigh unto Me!
One of the reasons I created thee
Was to fellowship with Me!

Draw nigh unto Me,
Don't live your life from afar.
I am the vine, you are the branch,
Let Me teach you who you really are.

You have learned much from the world,
Now come learn of Me.
For My yoke is easy,
And My burden light on thee.

In Me dwells all the treasures
Of wisdom and knowledge.
You are in Me so you have access
To My wisdom in *My Spiritual College*.

For by My Holy Spirit,
I will guide you into all truth.
You will develop into a spiritual giant,
No longer a babe in Christ – no longer a youth.

You will be a skilled workman:
Rightly dividing the Word of Truth,
A mighty tool in the hand of the Spirit.
A scheme of the enemy? You'll no longer fear it.

As you draw nigh unto Me,
I'll burn away all the chaff,
You'll dwell in My all consuming fire,
We'll look down at the enemy and laugh.

Scripture References:
James 4:8, Matthew 11:28-30, John 16:13, Hebrews 5:12-14
John 15:4-6, 2 Timothy 2:15, Colossians 2:1-3, Psalm 37:12-13

The Fight Of Faith

Against whom are you fighting,
The enemy or the fight of faith?
The enemy is already defeated,
It is your own mind you have to keep safe.

I said fight the good fight of faith,
That's what your armor is designed for-
Not fighting devils all day,
But in your mind the strongholds of war.

Tear them down
One by one.
Doubt, Fear, Unbelief,
Become a victorious son.

Oppression, Depression and **Worry**,
Probably the hardest of all to overcome.
Yet and still this victory
Must be won!

Cast down imaginations,
Always protect your head.
Instead of the hat of worry,
Don the helmet of salvation instead.

Scripture References:
1 Timothy 6:12, Ephesians 6:10-18, 2 Corinthians 10:4-6

Faith Is Your Servant

Faith is your servant
As you are My servant.
As you obey Me,
Faith works for thee.

Did I not say in My Word
Submit yourself to Me?
Then resist the devil,
Then he will flee from thee.

For obedience is the key
That unlocks the door of faith for thee.
Be obedient to walk in love.
Be obedient to banish unbelief.

Make your faith work,
Don't let it rest.
Make it work until it is finished,
Make it bring you My best.

Don't let it come in from the field.
Tell it to grid itself and serve you your meal.
Tell it not to expect thanks when the job is done.
That's what I made it for,
To serve you My son.

It starts out mustard seed small,
But it grows when spoken.
It grows when exercised,
So keep your mouth open.

Scripture References:
Luke 17:1-10, James 4:7, Matthew 17:20

Release Your Faith

As the Spirit of the Lord
Hovered over the deep,
His Power was just waiting,
Waiting for someone to speak.

Then God released His faith,
And he said, "**Light Be!**"
The Spirit's power kicked in,
Darkness had to flee.

This is the God-kind of faith
That Jesus used on the fig tree.
This is the God-kind of faith
That's available to you and me.

When like a flood,
The enemy dares try to come in.
Release the power of the Holy Spirit;
Lift up a standard against him.

Put him to flight!
Walk in the light!
You are the redeemed of the Lord.
It is your **New Covenant Right**!

Scripture References:
Genesis 1:2-3, Romans 10: 9-10, Mark 11:12-21, 22-25
Acts 1:8, Isaiah 59:19,59

The Blessed Path

Walk in the path
That I have prepared.
From a lot of unnecessary trials
In your life you will be spared.

For I have chosen you,
For such a time as this,
To do a work for Me,
A work that will not miss.

For it will hit its mark
And accomplish what I plan.
To tear down many strongholds
That are prevalent in the land.

It will also expose the error,
That has been taught by some,
And set My people free,
Free to grow to what I desire they become.

It will build and plant the truth,
The truth of My Word.
It will be confirmed by the Holy Spirit,
As the voice of My Word is heard.

So get on with the work,
Let's get this thing done.
The battle is **NOT** yours,
It's Mine and it's already won.

Scripture References:
Isaiah 30:21, Jeremiah 1:10, Isaiah 35:8-10

My Glory Is Upon Thee

My glory is upon thee;
You receive it while in My presence.
It comes along after you worship;
It is in fact part of My essence.

I bestow it upon thee for service:
To help you minister to others,
To better reach the world,
Your long lost sisters and brothers.

I bestow it upon thee for service:
To help the *Body of Christ*,
To strengthen the *Army of God,*
So they'll be willing to pay the price,

To discipline themselves like a soldier,
To win the battles of life,
To walk in love to protect the glory,
To avoid at all costs the entrance of strife.

My glory is upon thee,
Let it shine that others may see.
That power that is working through you,
Is really Christ living in thee.

Scripture References:
John 17: 20-23, 2 Timothy 2:3-4

Mustard Seed Faith

If you had faith as a seed,
Then you would say,
***"Be thou removed
And it must obey."***

For it has no choice,
To My Word you've given voice.
Hold your head up,
Receive and rejoice!

Scripture References:
Matthew 17:20

Power Of The Tongue

For the tongue carries death,
And the tongue carries life.
Make sure yours is not poisoned
By bitterness and strife.

When you discipline your tongue,
An increase in power will come.
I can't turn it up now,
To control your tongue-you must learn how.

Start by renewing your mind to My Word.
This will set your thoughts aright:
Pray in the Spirit,
Activate the Greater One in you,
Be strong in the Lord,
And the power of His might.

Scripture References:
Proverbs 18:21, Romans 12:1-2, Ephesians 6: 10, Jude 20

The Battle Rages On

The battle rages on!
The battle rages on!
Victory must be won!
Victory must be won!

As Moses held up holy hands
To turn the tide of battle for Israel.
You now lift up holy hands
To bring victory for God's people.

For holy hands of praise
Lifted up on high,
Means you surrender to Me
And I bring victory over your enemy.

Your hands and your voice
Both lifted up-
Create an atmosphere of habitation.
I will come to you and sup.

Scripture References:
Exodus 17:9-14, Psalm 8:2, Matthew 21:16, Psalm 22:3-4

I Will Perfect That Which Concerns Thee

I will perfect that which concerns thee.
I will perform My Word to you.
It will not return to Me void,
For it is tried, faithful and true.

Do not fret about this house,
I have everything under control.
Do not carry this burden,
On Me - your care you must roll.

Thank Me and Praise Me,
For what I have done.
Don't live a stressful life,
Relax and have some fun.

Learn to laugh at the devil
When he brings things your way,
I establish the end from the beginning.
My Word always has the final say.

Scripture References:
Psalm 138:8, Isaiah 46:8-10, 1 Peter 5:5-7, Psalm 2: 1-5

Be Anxious For Nothing

Be anxious for nothing.
Be anxious for nothing.
Don't carry this load,
Something inside will explode!

I did not design you
To carry the cares of life.
I designed you to roll them on Me,
Both you and your wife.

You have no overload switch.
You have no built in circuit breaker.
I designed you a care roller-
NOT a caretaker!

Let this thing go!
I told you that before.
I have it in My hand.
You have to trust Me, My man.

I know what I am doing.
I will surely bring you out.
Instead of sitting around worrying,
Rejoice with the **Victory Shout**!

Scripture References:
Philippians 4:4-7

Are You Half Dressed?

Choose this day
The clothes you will wear.
The rags of a prisoner complete with ball and chain
Or the *Armor of a Warrior,*
Ready to inflict some pain?

For your tongue activates your clothing,
You're either half dressed or dressed to kill.
It also influences your emotions.
You're either happy as a lark or you're a pill.

What you say surrounds you,
Get on you and gets in you.
Why would you say what the devil says?
Why accept the trash he sends you?

Activate your *Armor*
By declaring you have it on.
Decree each piece by name,
It's power to you **now claim**!

It works when you say it does.
It's My Armor, I ought to know.
Don't start your day half naked,
Get dressed before you go!

Scripture References:
Ephesians 6:10-18, Matthew 12:37, John 6:63, Psalm 109:17-19

The Harvest is Plenty

The **harvest** is plenty
But the laborers are few.
Why do you sit back?
Why do you not know what to do?

You have been diligent to sow:
Over many years you have sown.
The **harvest** is ready,
For your many seeds have grown.

They have grown into trees
With fruit ready to pick.
This is the fruit abounded to your account,
It is ripe, fat, and thick.

As you have labored to sow,
Now be diligent to reap.
Release the angels as reapers,
The **harvest** is yours to keep.

Say to them now:
"Go forth Heavenly hosts,
Gather the **harvest** into my hands."
For are they not all ministering spirits,
Ministering for the saved man?

Do they not harken
To the voice of My Word?
Do not keep silent,
Let My Word be heard.

They are enforcers of My covenant,
Angelic Sheriffs if you will.
They'll bring back stolen property,
They'll see that you get
What's in My Will.

Harvesting is not one day,
It is a season in time.
Get going – be aggressive,
They will bring you what is Mine.

Their activity has been accelerated;
There are more of them now on the earth.
They are ministers for the heirs of salvation,
For the children of the **New Birth**.

Scripture References:
Matthew 9:37-38, Mark 4:26-29, Psalm 103:20-21
Hebrews 1:14, Hebrew 2:1-3, Deuteronomy 33:2

Heaven's Resources

You have all of Heaven's resources
Available at your command.
Doubt, fear, unbelief and worry
Should not even be named in your land.

All of God's promises
In Me are yes and amen.
With that kind of backing,
How can you not help but win?

I knew what you would need
Before the foundation of the world.
That's why I put them there,
Each great and priceless pearl.

You don't have to beg,
For I have already said, "Yes."
Each and every one of them is yours,
Because you, I desire to bless.

Don't come to Me hoping
That I will say, "Yes."
If you found it in My Word,
It's yours already – **Be Blessed**!

I said, *"Come boldly to My Throne*
In the time of need,
That you may receive
Not beg and plead."

Whether or not you receive
Doesn't depend on Me.
I've already said, "Yes."
But what do you believe?

Bring Me to remembrance
Of My Word.
Ask Me in faith believing
That you I have heard.

From that moment on
You consider it done.
Though it looks like the battle rages,
The **Victory** has been won.

Call those things that be not
As though they already **were**.
This is the connection
That causes the manifestation to occur.

Scripture References:
Romans 4:17, Matthew 6:32, Hebrew 4:14-16
2 Corinthians 1:18-20, Matthew 7:7-8

Lo! I Am With You

Lo, I am with you,
Even unto the end of time.
I will never leave you nor forsake you,
After all, aren't you Mine?

Because you don't feel Me,
Doesn't mean I am not there.
Lo, I am always with you
Because I love you and I care.

Me and My Word are one.
Abide in Me and My Word in you.
Ask what you will,
And it will be done.

If you have My Word,
Then you have Me.
Go by what My Word says,
Not by what you see.

Stop going by your feelings,
They change everyday.
Remain constant in the Word,
It will show you the way.

In the beginning was the Word.
The Word was with God.
The Word was God.
I AM the Word!

My angels hearken
To the voice of My Word.
Whether it be from Me
Or from one of My saints it be heard.

I watch over My Word to perform it,
It upholds all things in your life.
Use it to calm the storms,
To keep away stress and strife.

Me and My Word are one,
You cannot separate one from the other.
Take My Word and use it.
Believers must help one another.

I uphold all things
By the Word of My power.
I expect you to do the same.
Use the sword of My Word,
The power of My Blood, and
The authority of My Name.

Scripture References:
Hebrew 13:5-6, John 1:1-5, 14, Jeremiah 1:9-11
John 15: 4-7, Psalm 103:20-21, Hebrew 1:1-4

I Gave You My Word

I gave you My Word,
The same Word that you've heard.
I AM the Lord, I change not.
Why My son, so quickly you forgot?

Did I not say,
You're not in this alone?
I still run this earth,
I'm still on the throne.

Get up and get going,
There is much work to do.
I am always beside you,
I will always see you through.

Don't get caught up
In what's going on.
Focus on what you have to do,
Stay prayed up and stand strong.

I have many plans
And things for you to do.
This is just a step,
A level to pass through.

Don't camp here,
It gets better down the road.
Don't carry this burden,
But on Me cast your load.

Humble yourself under My hand,
Together we go forth to possess the land.
I will exalt you in due time,
Speak My Word when tempted to whine.

My angels are with you,
Listening to what you say.
Give them something to work with,
Instead of listening to unbelief all day.

You give them
What I gave you-
A rhema Word,
It's tried, tested and true.

The Word will work
When you work the Word.
So work the Word,
The same Word that you've heard.

Scripture References:
Malachi 3:6, Jeremiah 29:11, 1 Peter 5:5-7, Psalm 103:20-21,
Isaiah 55:10-11, Psalm 18:28-30

The Spoils Of War

The wealth of the world
Is available to My child.
It does not come to the timid,
The weak, passive or mild.

It comes to the strong,
It is called the spoils of war.
You must be active and aggressive,
To receive what's in store.

The Kingdom suffers violence,
Violent men take it by force.
You have the right to use your faith,
After all, I am your source.

Be violent with your thoughts;
Don't bow to stinking thinking.
Take those thoughts captive,
Press on without even blinking.

Be specific with each transaction,
Identify each by name.
Keep records – times, dates, logs.
Keep a journal of each extraction.

Put in the sickle,
The harvest is ripe.
My angels will work for you,
If you'll just speak right.

Don't say what you feel.
Don't say what you see.
Say what My Word
Has revealed unto thee.

Scripture References:
Proverbs 13:22, Isaiah 55:10-12, Matthew 11:11-12
2 Corinthians 10:3-6, Ephesians 6:10-17, Hebrews 1:14
Proverbs 27:23-24

Think Like Me

Come up, come up, come up
with Me.
Come up from where you are,
Come up with Me and see,

The plans that I have for you,
To give you a future and a hope.
Plans to prosper you and bless you,
And take your vision to a larger scope.

Come sit with Me,
In Heavenly places.
Pull away from the busyness,
Get refreshed at this desert oasis.

I desire you to ride
Upon the high places of the earth.
I paid a great price for you-
You don't even know how much you're worth!

Think like I think,
After all, don't you have My mind?
You're made in My image and likeness,
You're made after My same kind.

The more time you wait before Me,
The more you become like Me.
Changed into My image from glory to glory
As I pour out the revelation of My story.

Think like I think,
And you become like Me.
As a man thinks in his heart,
So is he!

You can go as far
As your mind will allow in this hour.
Wallowing in unbelief,
Or soaring like the eagle with faith and power.

Come up, come up, come up,
And seeeeeeeeeee-
Just how high you can live
When you think like Me.

Scripture References:
Isaiah 55:1-11, Ephesians 2:1-10, Matthew 11:28-30, 1 Corinthians 6:20
Jeremiah 29:11-14, 1 Corinthians 2:12-15
2 Corinthians 3:17-18, Proverbs 23:7

Get Help Or Go It Alone

You can get help
Or you can go it alone.
I still run this earth.
I'm still on the throne.

You have chosen My help.
You chose not to go alone.
Yes, I still run this earth.
Yes, I'm still on the throne.

I will never leave thee
Nor forsake thee,
Yes, I'm always there.
You must learn to cast those burdens.
You must learn to roll your cares.

You desire to work and be blessed.
You desire to work without stress.
So roll the care on Me
And see yourself carefree.

You must see it to walk in it.
Remember, My promises are yes and amen.
Think like one who walks as a son-
Not like one who walks in sin.

Think like an heir
With an inheritance so rare,
Receiving all the promises,
Casting all you care.

You are not in this alone.
You have Me on the throne.
Think like one who is blessed.
Let go ALL forms of stress!

Scripture References:
Hebrew 13:5, Isaiah 41:10, Psalm 46:1, 1 Peter 5:6-7, Romans 8:16-17

Your Fears

I have addressed your fears
But you keep letting them slip.
Sometimes your mind's renewed,
Other times you let it dip.

It dips down into unbelief,
And stays there too long.
You allow it to become a thief,
You become weak when you should be strong.

For unbelief robs you of blessing,
And it robs you of My peace.
Dwelling on fears is a practice
That immediately must cease.

Your body knows no difference
Between the imagined and the real.
It reacts to what you dwell on,
Your health you can allow it to steal.

Dwell on what I say,
Meditate it night and day.
This will keep you in perfect peace,
If you choose to think this way.

Catch yourself when you dip.
Don't let the Word I've spoken to you slip.
Repent, then speak My Words over your life.
Cast down fears, anxieties, worries and strife.

Scripture References:
Isaiah 41:10, Isaiah 26:3, 1 Peter 5:7-9 Proverbs 23:7, Romans 8:15, Psalm 1:1-3

Expecting To Receive – 2

You must be expecting to receive
That for which you have believed.
Then your faith will conceive,
And deliver so that you do receive.

For faith is like a magnet,
When you expect, you attract.
Keep it turned on always,
It's your servant, it should not slack.

Keep blessings moving toward you,
Don't shut down when you receive one.
There is no limit to My supply,
My children are highly favored of the Son.

Follow the transaction
All the way to completion.
Don't stop because you don't see,
I will watch My Word to perform it.
You can always depend on Me.

Scripture References:
Acts 3:1-7, Luke 17:5-10, Isaiah 55:10-11

Simplify Your Life

Simplify your life!
Simplify your life!
Then understanding will come,
Both to you and your wife.

Your minds are too cluttered
With all sorts of things,
How can you hear from Me?
How can you receive what I bring?

Your minds are filled
With all worries and concerns.
With all I've been teaching you
Have you **not yet learned**?

Let those things **GO**!
I told you that before.
I have them in My hand.
I will complete My plan.

Give Me those concerns,
Then leave them with Me.
I will work them out.
Just you watch and see.

Scripture References:
Matthew 11:28-30, Luke 10:38-42, Philippians 4:6-8, Psalm 119:130

The Unsearchable Riches of Christ

The unsearchable riches of Christ
Are put there for the Body of Christ.

But no one takes the time-
No one makes the sacrifice-
To sit before Me and wait
And receive all that I have.

They rather rush out and not be late,
To go about with nothing on their plate.

I have prepared a table,
But no one wants to come.
I have invited all,
But in attendance, I only find some.

I have prepared a feast
Of everything you need.
But from the greatest to the least,
No one wants to heed.

No one wants to come,
No one wants to sit and feed.
All are leary of Me,
And that bothers Me indeed!

I am only here to help,
To give you life and to guide.
If only you will sit and wait,
And in My presence abide.

Then you will hear
The answers you have been seeking.
Then your way you'll see clear,
Instead of going forward just peeking.

Receive of Me.
For I AM free.
It only costs you your time,
But after all, isn't that also Mine?

Scripture References:
John 15:5, Isaiah 40:29-31, Ephesians 3:8-10, Luke 14:15-24

Restoration

Stand up and be bold.
Let your story be told.
Take back from the enemy,
Every penny, "7-Fold."

This is the time of restoration
For all in the Body of Christ.
It's time to get mean.
Stop being so nice.

Treat him like he is-
A liar and thief.
Take back what is yours
Says your Commander-In-Chief.

Go after it and get it,
According to Proverbs 6:30 and 31.
Make him restore all 7 times over.
Show him you're a son, a chosen one.

He has to give it back.
My angels enforce the Word.
Speak forth the restoration-
Let your voice be heard.

Scripture References:
Proverbs 6:30-31, Psalm 103:20-21, Joel 2:25

Turn Up The Power

I want to turn up the power
In the Body of Christ in this hour.
But, they have to watch their walk
And they have to watch their talk.

For My power comes as a sword,
A two-edged one at that.
It will definitely hurt the enemy
And it will also knock you flat.

Don't get careless in your walk
Or you will lose the power.
Don't get careless with your words
Or you'll cut yourself tomorrow.

For when I turn it up-
If you say the wrong thing,
The power is still active
And what you say it still brings.

So grow up in your walk
And grow up in your words.
Control the power
As your voice is heard.

Say what you want;
Don't say what you see.
I watch over My Word.
I will perform it for thee.

Scripture References:
Proverbs 18:21, Matthew 12:37, Hebrews 4:12, Jeremiah 1:12

Start With Me

Start your day with Me,
And all will go well.
I'll alert you to the enemy,
All the tricks and traps of hell.

For I desire you to be successful,
To walk in My plans and pursuits.
I do not want you to stumble,
To fall victim to his ruse.

So get with Me daily,
Preferably early.
I'll guide your steps all day,
To keep them from going squirrely.

Your footsteps shall be ordered,
Your pathway shall be bordered.
With angels encamping all around,
Rejoice with a praising sound.

Scripture References:
Matthew 6:33, Ephesians 6:10-11 Psalm 37:23-24
Psalm 34:7, 2 Chronicles 15:2-4, Jeremiah 29:11-14

Surgical Precision

With surgical precision,
You should be using My Word.
You should be putting into practice
Everything you've heard.

Did I not say
Be diligent and show thyself approved,
Rightly dividing My Word,
And not being so easily moved?

Precision comes through practice,
The more you use it, the better you get.
Begin wielding the **Sword of the Spirit**,
Speak the Word instead of frets.

It is alive and powerful,
Penetrating into joints and marrow.
It goes down deep
With the accuracy of an arrow.

In the Word of Righteousness
Become highly skilled.
The Holy Spirit will back you up,
In Him be continually filled.

Scripture References:
Hebrews 4:12, 2 Timothy 2:15, Hebrews 5:12-14

Rest In Me

You must learn to rest in Me,
Not in what you see.
I establish the end from the beginning-
Look not at the score in the middle innings.

It will turn our allright,
Walk by faith and not sight.
My hand is upon you.
This thing will NOT overrun you!

Rest in the Word-
I'LL NEVER LEAVE YOU NOR FORSAKE YOU.
Keep your eyes on Me
And see where I will take you.

As I was with Joshua,
So I'll be with thee.
Only be strong and courageous
And tell the spirit of fear to flee.

Scripture References:
Hebrews 3:7-19, Hebrews – Chapter 4
Joshua 1:4-5, Psalm 37:7, Isaiah 28:11-12

Feed My Lambs

Feed My Lambs!
Feed My Lambs!
They're starving for the Word.
They're being fed many scams.

They need good shepherds
Who teach what is right.
They need to be grounded
And walk in the light.

My Word is a lamp-
A lamp and a light,
An illumination in the darkness.
So they walk by faith, not by sight.

They need the Word
As often as they can.
They need the Word
So they can learn to stand.

Scripture References:
John 21:15-17, 1 Timothy 4:6-7, 1 Peter 5:2-4

Lo! I Am With You – 2

Lo, I am with you,
Even unto the end of time.
Lo, I am with you,
O precious child of mine.

I'll never leave you nor forsake you.
Don't think you're in this alone.
I see everything that's happening
As I watch here from My throne.

The race is not to the swift
Nor the battle to the strong.
Victory comes from Me-
Abiding in Me is where you belong.

Don't stray away
But **stay with Me closely**.
Follow My direction,
Instead of erring so grossly.

Get with Me, get refreshed,
Get renewed and strengthened.
I will multiply your days,
Your life I will lengthen.

Scripture References:
Matthew 28:18-20, Psalm 33:13-19, Psalm 91:1, 14-16
Psalm 2:1-4, John 15:1-7

I Am With Thee

Lo, I am with you,
Even unto the end of time.
Lo, I am with you,
O precious child of Mine.

Don't look around in fear
At all the things you see.
Despite what's going on,
My Presence goes with thee.

You have My **Grace**
Which is sufficient for thee.
You have My **Wisdom**
Which will enlighten thee.

You have My **Strength**
Which is made perfect in weakness.
You have My **Word**
Which lights your path in darkness.

You have My **Truth**
Which dispels all the lies.
You have My **Name**
Which no enemy can defy.

I did not design you
To walk in that limited way.
I designed you to live supernaturally,
Take time for Me, My Word and to pray.

Scripture References:
Matthew 28:18-20, 2 Corinthians 4:16-18, 2 Corinthians 12:9
James 1:5, Psalm 119:105, 130, James 1:17-18
1 Corinthians 2:12-16

My Perfect Will

My perfect will is
For you to be set free.
My perfect will is
For you to be debt free.
Be loosed from all
The entanglements of the world.
For your daily needs,
You come to Me.

I will supply your need
Above all you could ask.
Come to Me in faith believing-
That is your task.

I take care of My children.
I will not forsake My own.
Don't run down to the creditor
And take out that deadly loan.

Live above the ways of the world.
Live your Kingdom privileges now.
Learn how Kingdom finances work.
I will show you how.

Don't get buried in monthly bills.
You don't need Me to do that.
Bring your requests to Me.
I will supply, that is a fact.

The only "monthly bills" you should have
Are tithes and offerings to Me.
They open the ***Windows of Heaven***,
For Me to pour out blessings on thee.

Scripture References:
Philippians 4:19, Romans 8:12-17, Malachi 3:8-11
Romans 12: 1-3, Romans 13:7-8

The Work Of Your Hands

I have blessed the work of your hands
As I have brought you to this land.
I did not bring you here to leave you.
Lo, I am with you always.
Don't let the enemy deceive you.

I have plans for you-
To prosper you and give you hope.
Don't give into feelings that
You're at the end of your rope.

The footsteps of a good man
Are ordered of the Lord.
Don't think I'm not with you.
You and I are in one accord.

I will **NEVER** leave you nor forsake you.
I am here to help you.
Trust in My Word-
Not in what you have heard.

My plans and purposes
Will not be denied.
My Word is sure.
It has been tested and tried.

Put faith in My Word-
Say what I say.
Take authority over your work
Each and everyday.

Use My Word.
Use My Name.
Walk in My promises,
Every one that you claim.

Scripture References:
Hebrew 13:5-6, Deuteronomy 28:8,12, Jeremiah 29:11
Psalm 37:23, Isaiah 55:10-11, 2 Corinthians 1:19-20

Receiving Jesus as your Lord and Savior

As you have read through these poems, you may have been edified, exhorted, comforted and experienced victories through them, but have not received Jesus as your Lord and Savior.

Now is the time to take the **MOST IMPORTANT** step in your life and ask Jesus to be your Lord and Savior.

WHY? He forgives you of all your sins and is the ONLY guarantee that you will spend eternity in HEAVEN.

"For all have sinned, and come short of the glory of God…" Romans 3:2

HOWEVER…..

"That if thou shalt confess with thy mouth the Lord Jesus, and shalt believe in thine heart that God hath raised him from the dead, thou shalt be saved." Romans 10: 9-10

So….pray this out aloud:

"Dear God, I thank you for forgiving me of my sins. I receive Jesus as my Lord and Savior. I believe you raised Him from the dead. I thank you that I am now saved.

Welcome to the Family of God

The Body of Christ

About the Author

David Scott, II, born and raised in Savannah, GA, grew up in the Baptist Church. While in Louisiana, he encountered a business failure that caused him to seek the Lord for solutions. Not only did he receive solutions for the business, he received prophetic poems, the Word of the Lord, for all areas of life.

David now lives in San Antonio, TX with his wife and son. He is a Field Manager for a large industrial supply corporation. During his spare time, he enjoys watching sports, reading self improvement books, and working out at the gym. As a Toastmaster, he spends time improving his speaking and leadership skills. He is a member of Cornerstone Church with Pastor John C. Hagee where he serves as a Sunday School teacher.

APPENDIX

M.U.B.A. Worksheet
(Meditate, Understand, Believe, Act)

Things you will need to study the poems:
Bible, Pen/pencil, 3 ring binder, Copies of the M.U.B.A. worksheets

Instructions:

1. *Make copies of the M.U.B. A. worksheets and place in your 3 ring binder.*

2. *Select the poem you want to **M.U.B.A.**.*

3. *Read it aloud, slowly and **Meditate** (ponder, think on, speak) the words*

4. *Underline words that speak directly to you*

5. *Take each scripture at the bottom of the page and locate them in the Bible*

6. *Read them aloud, slowly and **Meditate** (ponder, think on, speak)*

7. *Begin to make notes about the words using the M.U.B.A worksheet*

8. *Begin to **Understand** these words and how they pertain to your situation*

9. ***Believe** the word and*

10. ***Act** on the word to receive the victory outlined in the poem*

M.U.B.A. Worksheet
(Meditate, Understand, Believe, Act)

Title of Poem _____

Scriptures/ Personal Notes/ Action(s) to be taken

_____

_____

_____

_____

_____

_____

_____

_____

_____

_____

_____

_____

_____

_____

_____

_____

_____